WOMEN AT WORK

WOMEN AT WORK

SUCCESSFUL TIPS
FOR WORKING TOGETHER

REBECCA CASSIDY

NEW DEGREE PRESS

WOMEN AT WORK

SUCCESSFUL TIPS FOR WORKING TOGETHER

ISBN   978-1-63730-826-4 *Paperback*
          978-1-63730-888-2 *Kindle Ebook*
          978-1-63730-962-9 *Ebook*

*"We will surely get to our destination
if we join hands."*

—AUNG SAN SUU KYI

*thank you for
reading my book!
Rebecca
Cassidy*

CONTENTS

———

INTRODUCTION

"I tell women that whole 'you can have it all'—mmm, nope, not at the same time. That's a lie. It's not always enough to lean in because that s*** doesn't work."
—MICHELLE OBAMA.

I was desperately trying to move out of my current job. The effect it was having on my mental health was crushing. I commuted an hour per day to work, sat alone in an office most of the day with rare human interaction, responded to angry emails, and updated the same spreadsheets over and over again. Then I sat in traffic for an hour—on a good day— to complete the thirteen-mile commute home, only to repeat the whole affair the next day.

After a year of this grind, I had become depressed and unfocused, which led to uncharacteristic mistakes. These lapses led to more frustration and depression and without anyone around me at work to bounce ideas off or even to have lunch with, I mentally and emotionally began to spiral.

I soon realized this work environment was not good for me, nor was it going to change anytime soon without any action on my part. I began applying to jobs at similar organizations in the area, but to little avail. After several months of applications, I received an interview invitation response from just one organization, but it was my top choice, my aspirational employer—my stretch school, if you will.

While there were a few downsides to the opportunity, this new job was at an organization that offered day-to-day variety in responsibility, the potential for career progression, and at its core, day-to-day human interaction and responsibilities beyond just spreadsheet work.

I wanted this job. *Desperately.*

So I interviewed. And interviewed. And interviewed. Three rounds of interviews with eleven different people later, I received an email with an informal offer outlining the title and salary. The email ended with, "Are you still interested?"

Hell yeah, I was interested! I was so excited. Excited to move out of my current situation, excited to move into an environment that was surely better for my health and my career. So, I took the next step as instructed by all the women-in-business books I had read: I began negotiating my salary.

The salary being offered was the same as I received at my current job, so it certainly wasn't unacceptable. *But I'm worth more, right? If I'm not going to control my own financial destiny, then who is? Girl power!*

So, I asked for 5 percent more than the offer, willing to meet somewhere in the middle. Plus, the director I was interacting with was a woman—the person I had interviewed with multiple times, the person who would be my boss's boss. Surely, she'd respect my willingness to negotiate.

Nothing could have prepared me for the next email she sent me.

"I'm sorry, but we can't offer you the position at that salary. We may have something opening up in the future—we will be in touch."

I was crushed under the weight of those two sentences. Gone was my chance to move on, to start a career rather than just working a day-to-day job. There was no negotiation, no second chance. *Did I ask for too much money? Did I start negotiating at the wrong point in the process? Was I too pushy? Or were all the books wrong?*

After a day or two of tears, devastation, and bewilderment, I went back to the women-in-business books to figure out where I had gone so wrong. It appeared I had followed procedure. I must just have been really bad at this negotiation thing, plain and simple. Because if the tactics, printed in black and white for the whole world to see, didn't lead to the outcome they predicted, then it must have been me. Books must be correct, *right?*

There is a bit of a happy ending to this story.

I gave myself a couple of weeks to settle down, and on a whim, reached out to the director again to see if something else had opened, as she had hinted at in her last email. I was in luck—another role in the office had opened, and she asked me to come in for another conversation.

Huzzah!

I went in about a week later, had another "conversation," and was offered the role. Same title as before, same responsibilities, but the interesting part was the salary was lower than that fateful first offer. This time, I eagerly accepted the position without a peep.

Upon moving into this new organization, I began a journey of observation. This new office was comprised of all women, from the receptionist up through the director. It wasn't that I hadn't had women bosses or colleagues in the past; in fact, most of my supervisors up until this point had been women. And I like working with other women—it's my comfort zone. But this was the first time I had worked in an office that was *all* women.

I quickly learned that the rules for succeeding in this new environment did not follow the rules outlined in the women-in-business books. Despite my best efforts to conform, I continued to make missteps.

Negotiation was clearly different—I had already learned that the hard way. I tried to lean in by offering my opinions in staff meetings; I was told in no uncertain terms to pipe down. I wanted to start new programs and offerings as innovation and creativity were encouraged; I could do so as long as all credit was given to my director. I wanted to collaborate with others across the organization; I first needed permission from my director, and I was to copy her on all emails and keep her in the loop of all conversations.

Again, on paper it doesn't sound particularly crazy—a boss should know what is happening with her staff and what projects they are working on. But this felt different. I had originally attributed these "rules" to the director and her need for control, but when she left to move to her next organization, nothing changed. There just seemed to be an unwritten set of rules that everyone else knew but me.

I'm a business/leadership book junkie, so I kept consulting the women-in-business books to figure out what those rules were. What I found, though, was that the vast majority of the books were about women working in male-dominated environments, usually from the perspective of working in Silicon Valley.

That is all fine and good, but what about when your boss is a woman, or when your work environment is mostly women? With women now making up nearly 50 percent of the workforce (US Bureau of Labor Statistics, 2020), what should women do to succeed in a female-led or female-dominated environment? Is there a different set of rules that apply? And if so, what are those rules?

Determined to figure out the answers to these questions, I began my research with this hypothesis in mind:

The rules for success when working in a primarily female environment are different than those for women working in a primarily male environment.

I began talking to women who had worked with and for other women. I started by asking the question, "What was it like to work for your female boss/colleague/subordinate?" Unsurprisingly, the first stories I heard were about the stereotypes. The backstabbing, the gossiping, the bad behavior our society likes to highlight in everything from scholarly journals to reality TV.

So, I started asking different questions, pressing for stories about *successfully* working with other women. "Tell me about a time you worked for a woman, and it went really, really well? Tell me about a woman who has inspired you?" It was then I started hearing about the positive experiences.

The stories of women supporting each other in the workplace, of mentoring each other, sponsoring each other, and of being the new kind of leader our changing society needs today.

As I listened to these inspirational stories, I felt the need to share them, to highlight the positive. I wanted to give us, as women, the confidence to be ourselves but still work together in ways that are productive rather than destructive. I wanted to collect these anecdotes and share them in a way that not only spells out how women—and men—can work for and with women but can do so in a way that is satisfying and, dare I say, enjoyable. It was then that I knew I needed to write this book.

This book, then, is written for those women who are just starting out or who are in the middle of their careers and are a bit baffled by the environments they find themselves in. It's written for those who might find the women-in-business books less than helpful because they work in environments that are *not* Silicon Valley. And it's written for women who are frustrated with their current work environment and just want to learn how to get along with others to make their days a little bit easier to navigate.

How to Use This Book

My goal for this book is for you, dear reader, to use this book as a tool. A tool for you to learn how to work not only with the women in your organization who behave badly but also with those who set positive, aspirational examples of leadership. A tool for you to use to learn why the negative behaviors might exist, so you can make informed decisions on how to work with those women to navigate your own career. A tool to learn from those who have set positive examples so we might learn to be the leaders and supporters our work environments so desperately need today.

I want this book to be the one I was looking for earlier in my career when I was trying to figure it all out.

We will begin by exploring the history of women in the workplace. History matters, and without knowing our collective past we are doomed to repeat it. We must learn why women have earned the reputation they have, why the bad behavior exists, and how to deal with those who feel that the stereotypical bad behavior is still acceptable today.

We will then move into the research to discuss why women tend to tear each other down rather than build each other up. We will then review, from a sociological perspective, how groups of people function, and what tools members of these groups use to be successful within the group. We will look at how men and women use these tools differently as this difference is the foundation for success in female-dominated environments.

Finally, we will discuss each of the stereotypes we often hear about from the most difficult-to-work-with through "I've-hit-the-jackpot." Each chapter, beginning with chapter four, will describe a specific stereotype and why women might have developed such behavior. You will hear anecdotes from women about working for women in each of these categories. You'll learn why and how some of these behaviors have developed over time, and how we, as subordinates, coworkers, and leaders, can work with each other as human beings rather than as stereotypes.

You may find that you'll relate to some of the anecdotes and research in this book but not others. You may even read some of the stereotypes and say, "That describes my male boss." I, too, can say that about a few stereotypes. But in an effort to write just one book rather than a set of encyclopedias, I will stick to the archetypes I and my interview subjects have come across in our careers.

Think of this book as a lifeline for you throughout your career, when you find yourself working in wonderful or challenging situations. You may even find some advice in these chapters to help you become the best leader you can be. Finally, I will end each chapter with the following mantra: in the end, the only behavior you can truly control is your own.

My Disclaimer

Please also note my brief disclaimer that the lenses through which I write this book are specific to me and my experiences. The individuals I interviewed for this book span race, ability, and gender identities, but collectively are college-educated and are working or studying in primarily white environments. Finally, in the interest of simplicity in writing, I refer to two sexes: men and women, but with full acknowledgment that gender identity spans a wide spectrum and can add a whole layer of complexity to interpersonal work relationships, a topic for a whole other book.

So please, join me on this journey of discovery. I hope we can learn and improve together because a rising tide lifts all boats.

PART I

HOW WOMEN WORK

———

CHAPTER 1

HOW WE GOT HERE

"Society is wise in its generation. It realized not long ago that there were innumerable charming women within its fold who could work, and who were ashamed to beg. Consequently [society] said: 'We will approve the woman who works, provided she is a charming woman.' And society smiled, and working-women became many in number; and then people who did not understand, thought that this was a fancy that would soon die out. But it has not and it will not."

—RUTH ASHMORE, FROM *THE BUSINESS GIRL IN EVERY PHASE OF HER LIFE*, 1898

"You are so lucky to be growing up today. Back when I was growing up, women became teachers or nurses. Those were our only choices."

In that moment, I did feel lucky. It was sometime in the mid-1990s and I had bumped into my fourth-grade teacher at the local grocery store while home during a break from college. We were having the what-are-you-going-to-do-after-college conversation, and at the time I was considering a career as a physical therapist.

My teacher's response about my various career options really made me feel fortunate to be coming of age at that time. In that moment I truly believed I could do anything I put my mind to. Even as I write this, the "Free to Be You and Me" song that I played incessantly as a kid, rings in my head: "Anything you can do I can do better..."

It never occurred to me at that time that, from a historical perspective, the idea of women in the workplace was a relatively new construct. I had naively assumed that like me, all women followed a similar prescribed path: graduate high school, then college, get a good job, and experience similar success as men. The end. I thought that following this path was just what one did, irrespective of gender.

And for the most part, I did follow that path. I went to high school and then college. My first job out of college was in consulting, and for the most part my teams were fairly evenly mixed, gender-wise. Perhaps slightly more male leaning, but not so much that I ever felt like I was in the minority.

After four years of working, I began my graduate education in business school, during which time I became hyperaware of my gender. I was very much in the minority in my classes and felt as though it was my responsibility to represent the whole of women. But I got used to it. I figured out the norms of business school, of working with men, of being in the minority, and learned to go along to get along.

A few years later I moved overseas to Asia and discovered a whole new set of norms. Working as a woman in a male-dominated society AND as a foreigner was very different from what I had become used to and made for some comical mistakes on my part. Walking into meeting rooms, I sat in chairs that were implicitly reserved for the highest-ranking member of the company; I was quickly "invited" to sit in a different chair. One time I hugged another woman when she announced her pregnancy; wrong thing to do. Another time I had forgotten to wear socks to a dinner at which shoe removal was required; bare feet at dinner are gross in any society. But again, I quickly learned from my mistakes by going along to get along. And despite my awkwardness and downright embarrassment, I look back upon that time fondly.

Three years later, I returned home to the US and began a career in higher education. I quickly found that the go-along-to-get-along strategy did not work as well as it had in the past. It took me a long time to pinpoint why I had such a hard time adjusting to my new working environment.

While I began recognizing patterns in unspoken expectations, it still took more mistakes and missteps than it had in previous settings to figure out how to best work beside others. But after a year or so, it hit me: for the first time in my life, I was working with nearly all women.

Upon this realization I began looking for guidance as to how to successfully work in this new all-female environment. I began with the women-in-business and women-in-leadership books but found them to be much more focused on how women can succeed in primarily male environments, specifically in Silicon Valley. It seemed that no one else had yet defined the rules for success for women working with other women, at least not in writing. I then started asking other women about their experiences in working with other women but heard mostly horror stories as opposed to helpful tips.

The good news is that eventually, I figured it out. Many of my lessons I've learned over the years are spelled out in this book, and despite the bumps in the road, I truly believe women are great to work with. Yes, I came across some stereotypes, but twelve years later, I'm still working in the same female-dominated environment and frankly, the women I work with are wonderful. I wouldn't trade it for anything.

That said, my experience has taught me women *do work differently*. Not in ways that are necessarily better or worse—just different. Men and women have the same set of tools at their disposal to function within the workplace. However, in researching this book, I have learned that women and men differ in the way that each gender *uses* these tools. Specifically, women differ in how they

- develop **trust** and **social capital,**
- use **self-disclosure** and **language,** and
- demonstrate **emotional intelligence.**

Once we understand and embrace how women use these tools, I believe women can enjoy their day-to-day work environment with each other. But before we explore how women work differently, let's look at the history of women in the workplace and how we got to where we are today.

History of Women in the Workplace

In the preindustrial eras of Western history, men and women often worked alongside each other in agricultural settings (Encyclopaedia Britannica Online Ed, 2021). The development of the Industrial Revolution in the late 1800s into the

1900s, particularly in Britain, transitioned entire families—men, women, and children—from working on farms to working in factories.

However, the treatment of women and children in factories was often horrific. So horrific that Britain and other countries in the West passed minimum age and maximum working hours laws resulting in many women and children moving back to the homestead, leaving the paid workforce to be dominated by men.

As factory technologies developed during the Industrial Revolution, there became an increased need for a more educated workforce. A public education system developed, and while men filled the first teaching roles, they found they could make more money in factories. Women, particularly single women, filled the teacher shortages in the classroom.

It was World War II, however, that spurred true change both in American society and its workforce over the next several decades; changes that still affect us today. As men left to fight overseas, single and married women supported the war effort by filling the vacant factory positions. Upon men's return from the war, women either left their jobs to return to the home or were fired to give men back their jobs in the factories.

After working outside the home for several years, however, women's appetite for economic and social independence had been whetted. Economic scarcities during World War II in the US led women to save most of their earnings during the war. Thus, women had inadvertently saved money for down payments on homes, which in turn launched the boom years of the 1950s (US National Archives, 2016). In the 1960s, the development and subsequent legalization of birth control pills gave women the option to have more of a say in the number of children they would bear and therefore more choice as to whether or when to work (Nikolchev, 2016).

In 1969, California became the first state to enact a law saying that divorce could be granted for irreconcilable differences, called "no-fault divorce." States around the country followed suit, and newly single women found they *had* to work to support themselves and any children they had, keeping more women in the workforce (James, 1970). The Equal Credit Opportunity Act of 1974 banned banks from requiring a husband's signature for a woman to obtain a credit card, giving women further control over their finances. In 1978, the Pregnancy Discrimination Act disallowed employers from firing women simply for becoming pregnant. In the 1980s and into the 1990s, women entered the workforce at an increasingly rapid pace, not just because they had to, but because society was now saying it was okay to want to.

Women's participation in the workforce continued to climb and peaked in 1999, at which time, 60 percent of all women were working women (US Bureau of Labor Statistics, 2021). Participation has since leveled off and has even declined up through the start of the 2020 COVID-19 pandemic, for a variety of reasons that are subjects for other books. But in 2020, women made up 47 percent, or nearly half, of the entire workforce (McKinsey, 2020).

Moving Up the Corporate Ladder

Even with this powerful wave of women moving into the workforce, women today still work primarily at entry-level and mid-level management positions. In looking at McKinsey & Company's and LeanIn.Org's data gathered in 2020, the percentage of women in upper management and executive levels (sometimes referred to as the C-suite) drops dramatically. The contrast is starker for women of color with only 3 percent of C-suite positions being held by these women.

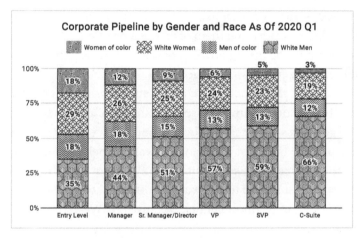

Data Credit: McKinsey & Company and LeanIn.Org, 2020

One would think the sheer numbers of women entering the workforce in the past eighty years would have pushed women up the ranks, resulting in fairly even percentages across various levels of corporate America. But the data show that not to be the case. Which leads us to the question, *why?*

Why would the percentages of women drop so drastically as we look to the higher levels of corporate America? Why haven't women made as much progress through the ranks as they have in simply entering the playing field?

Of course, moving up the ladder takes time and hard work. Keep in mind that people generally do not climb their career ladders in a vacuum. People of all genders must put in the work to make it to the next level in their career, but it also takes someone above them to give them a chance. Often called sponsorship, someone who has more power within a work environment can help someone at a lower level move up either by informing them of an open position, advocating for them in the hiring process, or outright hiring them into a higher position (Mobley, 2019).

We will talk much more about sponsorship in chapter ten, but for now, know that sponsorship is often done out of the goodness of one's heart. A sponsor will see something in the protégé they can relate to and want to help that person in their career. However, without any sort of guardrails in place, sponsors tend to advocate for others who are like them, most often in terms of gender. Because our Western society is male dominated, men often hold the seats of power and tend to sponsor other men in their careers. Men might see something in a male protégé that reminds them of themselves and want to help them avoid the mistakes and pitfalls they faced earlier in their careers (Ibarra, 2010).

Again, most of the time, this sponsorship is not out of a hatred for women nor is it even always a conscious decision. But these male-to-male sponsorships will lock women out of promotions, higher positions, and career growth. Add on race, ethnicity, and gender identity, and some women will find it nearly impossible to move up. Good intentions, misogynistic results.

Of course, this is not always true 100 percent of the time. Over the past eighty or so years, there have been many women who have made it to positions of leadership in organizations around the world due to their own hard work as well as to sponsorship by people above them. *But if that is the case, shouldn't they be helping those women who are coming up behind them? And if not, why not?*

Arianna Huffington laments in her book, *On Becoming Fearless*, women in the workplace are held to a variety of standards that often conflict with each other. "Be nice and demure and just hope that someone notices and gives you a promotion, or be assertive, get labeled as pushy and aggressive and hope you advance before becoming too hated. As most women know, it doesn't take too much to get labeled pushy and aggressive... Who is responsible for this double standard—men or women? However it began, the answer right now is both."

Anyone who has been to high school and has dealt with female cliques knows in her gut that Huffington is right. However, there is proof to back up her claims. It also may help explain why the ascent through the ranks of corporate America has been a tough one for many women.

Benevolent and Hostile Sexism

Regula Zimmermann and Pascal M. Gygax of the University of Fribourg, Switzerland, conducted a study published in 2015 that investigated why some women might be led to behave stereotypically badly and in some cases perpetuate sexist beliefs. In a study entitled "Women's Endorsement of Sexist Beliefs," the researchers built upon a 2010 study conducted by Julia Becker that investigated the concepts of benevolent sexism and hostile sexism. According to Becker, benevolent sexism is a statement about women that most people would not necessarily consider to be offensive, such as "Women are generally kind." Hostile sexism, then, is defined as a statement that assigns negative characteristics to women, such as "Women are too easily offended."

In Becker's study, women aged eighteen to twenty-four were asked to read through a series of statements that researchers classified as either benevolent or hostile sexism. The researchers used such benevolent phrases as "Women are morally sensible," and hostile phrases such as "Women exaggerate problems at work." Each woman in the study was then asked to determine if the phrases described herself as an individual or described a certain subgroup of women, which the researchers defined as housewives, career women, feminists, or temptresses.

What Becker found was that participants associated the benevolent phrases with themselves as individuals and with the subgroup they identified with. At the same time, they associated the hostile statements with the other subgroups. In this particular example, a career woman would associate the phrase "Women are morally sensible," with herself and other career women, but would associate the phrase "Women exaggerate problems at work," with the other subgroups that were not her own. Same held true for feminists, housewives, and temptresses. Each described herself and her own subgroup benevolently, while describing the other subgroups with hostility.

Zimmermann and Gygax then took this finding a step further and asked the question, would women assign the hostile sexist comments to *women as a whole* in addition to the other subgroups of women? To find out, they repeated Becker's study but added the option of assigning various phrases to women as a whole.

What they found was that women would assign the benevolent statements to themselves AND to women as a whole but would still assign the hostile statements to various subgroups of women with whom she did not identify. For example, the feminist attributed the benevolent statements to herself, feminists, and to women as a whole, but would attribute the hostile statements to housewives or career women (temptresses were removed from this part of the study). Same held true for career women and housewives.

The researchers continued to ask why. Why do women look upon themselves, their own subgroup, and women as a whole benevolently while still maintaining hostility for other subgroups of women? Why is a feminist okay with herself, other feminists, and with women altogether, but not with housewives?

The answer may lie in a psychological theory called "System Justification Theory."

System Justification Theory

We first must remember that humans in general are social animals and experience feelings of security when we are part of a group. There is safety in numbers. Back in the hunter-gatherer days, staying within a group and staying closest to the one(s) in power meant increased security: more access to food, shelter, human contact, and survival. Being shunned from the group decreased the chance of survival. Today, being shunned can happen within a family, a group of friends, or at a multinational corporation.

When we tie a theory called System Justification Theory to this idea of group-belonging-equals-survival, things start to make sense. System Justification Theory says that "members of disadvantaged groups would not engage in social change if their system justification motives were stronger than their ego and group justification motives" (Jost & Hunyady, 2005).

In other words, an individual or a group will do what it takes to keep their group closest to those in power to maintain their access to that power and safety. If an individual or a group perceives that the system they are in is working for her, then change is not necessary. That system could be the home, a workplace, a school, or society as a whole. Even if you aren't the one in power, you'll do what you can to maintain your current place in society as well as your access to power.

The upshot? If it ain't broke, don't fix it.

Going back to the benevolent and hostile sexism study, Zimmerman and Gygax then argue that based on System Justification Theory, the women participants in their study were content with their place in society, even if their place was not in power. Their access to resources and their psychological and physical safety were currently acceptable. They surmised that each woman respondent was comfortable with her access to power, was comfortable with her own subgroup's access to power, and was comfortable with her larger group's access to power.

However, the researchers theorized the women participants *were* concerned that other subgroups of women outside of her own might interfere and unseat them. Feminists may be subconsciously concerned with housewives or career women usurping their place in the order. Same for the housewives and same for the career women.

The solution to this problem is, then, to assign hostile statements to the other subgroups, pushing them away from those in power to maintain their own subgroup's perceived place in the order. Like crabs in a barrel, women are pulling each other down to stay closest to the group in power—men—in an effort to survive.

Applying System Justification Theory to the workplace may then explain why women will do what they can to reach the top of their company or organization but not necessarily help those behind her. Rising to the top requires a lot of emotional and intellectual effort, as well as social and political capital, for any gender. But women must spend more social capital to rise to the next level, as we will discuss in the next chapter.

Once a woman reaches a place of comfortable power or proximity to power in her career, she must then decide if she has enough social capital to "spend" to bring other women up to her level. If she does, she may decide to spend that capital to lift someone else up, *as long as she feels she can retain her place in the system.* If she feels she doesn't have the social capital to spend, or her proximity to power is too tenuous, she may choose to either ignore the women behind her or perhaps even distance herself from other women.

While this is just a theory, and much more research needs to be done, my gut says this is spot on. In thinking back to the director mentioned in the introduction, I know she had worked extremely hard to get to where she was at that time. But after learning about System Justification Theory for myself, I'm convinced she felt she couldn't trust the system to allow her to bring others up to her level without losing her own place within the system.

With consequences for helping others potentially disrupting access to power and safety, it's no wonder women are hesitant to help other women. But the purpose of this book is not to just explain why the bad behavior exists; it is to explain how we, as women, can surmount this bad behavior and help each other at the workplace without fear of consequences. Women have certainly helped others and have lived to tell the tale. It is up to use to learn how it's done so we can work peacefully alongside each other and help others rise along with us. In the next chapter, we will investigate just how some women have done so.

CHAPTER 2

SOCIAL CAPITAL
AND TRUST

———

"Add women and stir—that just doesn't work."
—ANALÍA GÓMEZ VIDAL, PHD, SOCIAL
SCIENCE RESEARCHER & COACH

Anyone who has taken any amount of coursework in business school likely had a group project. Depending on the class or the program, business school professors and administrators will lump students together in groups of four to six people for a semester or a year. People representing various gender identities, races, and ages are mixed into a group with the idea that if everyone learns how to peacefully work together with people unlike themselves in business school, then they will peacefully work together with people unlike themselves in the "real world."

In my second year of business school, I was placed in a group for a semester-long project. Among my five-person team were a Russian student and a Ukrainian student.

It did not go well.

I was at first puzzled as to why the Russian and Ukrainian would never sit next to each other during group meetings. Or why one would find an excuse to leave early if the other was there. Or why, later in the semester, one just stopped showing up to group meetings altogether.

Fast forward to 2014 when Russia invaded Ukraine, and it all made sense to me. The college administrators had failed to consider the team members' collective histories and values. They presumably didn't realize that each of these students carried with them a cultural and political history based on years of strife; they just saw one man and one woman and put them together on a team. They checked the gender diversity box and moved on.

Over the past few decades, employers have followed this same logic. If a company just hires more women, it will achieve gender parity, and everyone will live happily ever after. In fact, the 1980s and 1990s saw the highest number of women entering the workforce, not only because of cultural changes but due in large part to gender diversity initiatives in corporate America. As a result, by the year 2000, 60 percent of all women were in the workforce, a historical high (Vsource Blog, 2020).

What we, as a society, are beginning to realize, however, is that the "add women and stir" strategy isn't working. Simply hiring more women without considering women's histories and values is not going to result in happy workplaces—neither for men nor for women.

In a perfect world, when marginalized groups are brought into a new environment, the groups in power would take a moment to consider the new and current individuals' ways of working. Different groups have different histories that dictate how the members of each group should work together to achieve a goal. And to accomplish this shared goal, all groups of humans, regardless of where they are in geography and history, rely on one main social construct: social capital.

Social Capital

The Organization of Economic Cooperation and Development defines social capital as "networks together with shared norms, values, and understandings that facilitate co-operation within or among groups." When these networks are put together, they engender trust and "enable people to work together" (OECD 2020).

Based on the OECD's definition, social capital is the currency of groups of people. It is earned and spent, just like money. It is earned by doing things for other people within a specific group and is spent when you ask others to do things for you. And once spent, it is gone until you earn more.

But what happens when we can't earn social capital, or there is no one of whom we can ask favors? We hire people to do stuff for us and pay them cold hard cash to do it.

Let's say my lawn needs to be mowed. If I can't or don't want to do it, I can ask my spouse to do it. Since I have built up a lot of social capital with him, he will likely do it without asking for anything in return (depending on the day). If he can't or won't do it, then I would have to go to someone with whom I have less social capital, such as my neighbor. If she says yes and mows my lawn, I will likely have to return the favor at some point in the future. If my neighbor can't or won't do it, and there is no one else I can call on to do it for free, I'll have to pay someone in cash to do it. We spend financial capital when we have no social capital left to spend or we don't want to spend it on that task or person.

In my personal experience, I have found there are two important aspects to building social capital:

1. Social capital is specific to the social groups to which you belong.

Think about the different groups of people in your life. Those groups can include your family, your place of employment, your religious group, your neighborhood, etc. Now imagine asking someone within each of those groups for a favor. Then determine whether that person:

a) would do the favor without question,
b) would do the favor but would expect something in return,
c) would do the favor but you would have to present the return favor to them as part of the ask, or
d) would only do the favor in return for money.

The higher up on the options you were able to answer, the more social capital you have within that group. For some groups, you may have a lot of social capital and can get things done relatively easily by asking for and providing favors. For some groups, however, you may have very little social capital, and actual financial currency may be required to get things done.

This was me a few years ago.

I had been working at my employer for several years and had built up a solid network of people. People I could call on to answer questions, to help with projects, or for general support. Feeling comfortable at work, I decided to try to expand my social network and joined my kid's Parent Teacher Association.

I was new to this group and therefore had no social capital. Not only did I find that my balance of social capital within this group was zero, I also found I couldn't even open an account at this bank. I didn't know any of the other moms or dads and I found that none had any interest in getting to know me. I attended a few meetings and volunteered for a few positions only to receive a "thanks, but no thanks." Unless my actual financial cash was needed for fundraisers, my presence was irrelevant to the group's goals.

While my feelings were a bit hurt, I decided I had a choice. I could stick around and slowly begin the process of building social capital, or I could focus my time on my other social groups in my life. This brings us to our next point:

2. Building social capital takes time.

I knew that if I wanted to build my social capital within the PTA, I would have to spend A LOT more time reaching out to the other parents, getting to know them on a personal level, and doing favors for them outside of the PTA. But time is the great equalizer, and we all only have twenty-four hours in the day.

After some reflection, I decided I would rather spend my time and effort building and maintaining my social capital at work and within my family, my top two social groups. It wasn't something I had done consciously, but after several years at my employer, I had found that I could easily ask others for favors and I knew who I could and should do favors for.

If I did decide, however, that it was worth my time to build my social capital within the PTA, or any other group I was new to, I would then have to think about how I was going to build that capital.

How Social Capital Is Built

According to Robert Putnam, author of *Social Capital Primer*, social capital stems from trust, reciprocity, the sharing of information, and cooperation. Additionally, people will trust, reciprocate, share information, and cooperate among networks of relationships they have built within their organization. These networks are key to how people get work done, but men and women build these networks differently.

Women tend to develop relationships with others who are on the same rung of the ladder or in similar spots in the organizational hierarchy (Angervall, Gustafsson, and Silfver, 2018). These relationships, once built, are called horizontal networks. Women will develop these relationships by either sharing information (e.g., talking about their kids/pets/significant others), by building trust (e.g., "Don't tell anyone I told you!"), and through showing empathy (e.g., sending flowers for a death in the family).

Men, on the other hand, tend to build networks vertically with people above or below them. The methods may be similar: sharing information (e.g., forwarding information about job openings in other departments), building trust (e.g., working on a project together), and through showing empathy (e.g., signing the sympathy card that someone else arranged). But while men and women use the same methods to build their networks, the direction in which they build their networks results in different outcomes.

Social capital is "borrowed" from those higher in the organization and spent on those who are lower in the organization (Storberg-Walker, 2007). As a result, vertical networks tend to be more powerful in the workplace. Those who have access to these vertical networks—more often than not, men—tend to be the recipients of that social capital before those in horizontal networks, which tend to be women (Walby, 2011).

At the same time, horizontal networks tend to be more emotionally supportive. Women who have strong horizontal networks tend to be happy within their organization, even if they become frustrated with their lack of upward movement. "Building close relationships can be personally rewarding and provide emotional sustenance and support, both of which are important, especially for women who feel isolated in their jobs," says Sally Helgesen, author of the book *How Women Rise.*

But Helgesen also is of the opinion that horizontal network building for the sake of building relationships is a waste of time. "[But] if you steadfastly refuse to leverage the relationships you've built in pursuit of your goals, you will diminish your ability to reach your full potential. And that would be a shame." So, for those women who would like access to stretch projects, raises, and an upward career trajectory, vertical and horizontal network building is vital to the accumulation of social capital.

One woman I spoke with named Zoia, a VP at a global financial institution, worked in an all-female environment when she first moved to the US from Israel. "It was so much fun," she says. "There were conversations in the kitchen about SoulCycle classes, about meal prep, and just general camaraderie." While these random kitchen conversations likely felt like they were just fun for Zoia, they were actually very important in building Zoia's horizontal network. She still managed to build a vertical network, as we will find out soon, but for women horizontal networks can be a lifeline for mental health and social support, and building it is certainly not a waste of time.

But regardless as to whether networks are built vertically or horizontally, they are necessary to get work done. Even the most introverted of us still must work with customers, subordinates, colleagues, and bosses. And to work together toward a goal, we must, on occasion, spend the social capital generated within those networks.

How Social Capital Is Spent

Unfortunately for women, it can take a long time to build social capital, particularly in the workplace. As Lois Frankel says in her book *See Jane Lead*, "A woman's credibility doesn't follow her from successful achievement to successful achievement. She must prove herself with every challenge." As a result, it's very important to judiciously choose on whom we spend that social capital.

Frankel's comment brought me back to my conversation with Zoia. While she was working in her all-female environment, she was also volunteering for a nonprofit organization that supports women who work in innovation. Her supervisor asked her to develop a presentation for a Board of Directors' meeting with only a few days' notice. She started to panic. Given that Zoia just started volunteering with the organization, she still didn't have a good grasp on the organization's mission. When she asked her supervisor for a bit more guidance, the response was, "Take a stab, just do your best."

Her frustration built. She didn't know what to do or where to go and her supervisor didn't give her any path or guidance, but it turned out to be a good thing. "It forced me to spend time to think it through. So, I presented two options and made a list of specific questions. Then I took my ideas back to her. She taught me to create structure within ambiguity."

This process was the first step in Zoia earning social capital with her supervisor and gaining her trust. Later, Zoia developed a newsletter, a podcast, and grew the organization's followership sixfold, all at no additional cost to the organization's budget. When Zoia began applying to paying full-time positions, her supervisor became her biggest cheerleader and her sponsor. She made some personal calls and cashed in some of her own social capital on Zoia's behalf.

"[I think] I had done enough for her to want to go out on a limb and use her social capital," said Zoia. "But imagine if I had messed up in the interviews that she had recommended me for? It would have been very, very bad for her. She opened the door for me, because she knew when I got there, I would actually be a positive reflection on her. I think that's the beauty of working with women. I don't know if a man would have felt so comfortable as to lead me to the door."

Zoia's supervisor had watched Zoia prove herself while building this project. As a result, she was willing to go to the mat for her using some of her own social capital. She had built up enough trust with Zoia to know she was unlikely to make her look bad in future positions.

After all, no one wants to recommend someone for a project or position and then find out they have done a poor job. Women find this letdown very difficult to recover from. As Herminia Ibarra says in her article "A Lack of Sponsorship is Keeping Women from Positions in Leadership," "While an executive's store of knowledge will not be depleted if he or she shares it with someone else, the political capital he or she spends fighting for someone to get a key assignment can no longer be used on something else."

Social Capital and Trust

In the workplace—and in society—trust is everything. Social capital is built on trust. Recall that Putnam says social capital stems from trust, reciprocity, the sharing of information, and cooperation. Trust says that if I do you a favor, I believe you will return the favor (reciprocity). Trust says that if I give you a portion of my project, I believe you will do a good job on it and together we will both benefit (cooperation). Trust says that if I share information with you, I believe you will share information with me, or you will do what I want with that information (sharing of information). And if trust is broken, I will, in the future, spend exactly zero of my social capital on you.

When trust in the workplace is broken, an unfortunate, vicious cycle breaks out. Information becomes scarce, transparency fades, and a lack of sincerity develops. We then go into protective mode and prioritize our own psychological safety rather than focusing on the team's or organization's mission. A toxic environment then develops and thrives. This can happen in a group as small as two people or in a group as large as a nation.

I spoke with Marge, a former HR executive, who worked in female-dominated job settings for the majority of her career. For the past ten years, she worked for a pharmaceutical company that had a large European contingency, which added a layer of cultural difference to the gender tension in her office.

She relayed stories of executive women who insisted on being involved in every detail of projects, from formatting text and fonts for e-learning products to personally picking out gifts for the administrative assistants at holiday times. She felt that these executives were so involved in the details of other people's jobs that it hampered their ability to focus on actively leading their teams and organization.

When I asked Marge why these executives felt the need to control every minute detail, her opinion was that it all came down to trust, or a lack thereof. "There was no trust that I, with twenty years of experience in designing e-learning products, could in fact, work with the engineers myself on these products. There was no trust that other people could order the 'right' gifts for the administrative assistants," says Marge. In short, the executives did not trust that anyone else had their best interests in mind.

A team or organization will have a hard time achieving their mission and goals if the leaders are spending their time doing everyone else's work, which in turn can result in inefficiency, a lack of innovation, and low morale. And if you are reading this book, chances are you've been in an environment where trust has broken down.

How Trust Is Built

In the same way that men and women build social capital differently, researchers have found that men and women build trust differently. A study conducted by researchers at The Ohio State University in 2005 demonstrated how women and men decide who to trust.

In the study, men and women who were students at Ohio State were given the choice to receive three dollars from the researchers or to receive eleven dollars from a stranger. For those students who chose to receive the money from a stranger, they could decide if that stranger was from Ohio State or that stranger was at a different university where the student had a friend attending. In other words, they were a friend of a friend. There was no guarantee the students would receive the money from any of the strangers.

The researchers found that students, more often than not, chose to receive the eleven dollars from the stranger. However, what they also found is that the men and women in the study differed in which type of stranger they would trust enough to receive the money. The men more often chose to receive the money from the Ohio State stranger while women more often chose to receive the money from the stranger who was a friend of a friend.

These results show that men tend to trust those who belong to the same group of which they are already a part, whether that is the same university, same workplace, same fraternity, etc. Women, however, rely more on established relationships. Personal connections—friends, friends of friends, etc.—are more important than the group to which they belong. For women to build trust, they must get to know one another on a personal level. Or they must be connected somehow to someone they know. Women don't just trust anybody simply because they are in the same university, same workplace, etc. Women need to have the one-to-one relationship in place or need to know that someone they already trust in turns trusts the stranger. It's a one-to-one (-to-one) thing.

Women, Social Capital, and Trust

Once women know each other, building trust, and therefore social capital, among women is generally straightforward: do what you say, say what you do, and make your boss or coworker—and therefore yourself—look good. Know what is expected of you, ask questions if you aren't sure, and give it your best effort.

A reasonable woman will appreciate your efforts and will reciprocate, building the common trust within the group needed to succeed. But when trust is broken, social capital deteriorates, and things can go very, very wrong.

CHAPTER 3

HOW WOMEN WORK: BUILDING SOCIAL CAPITAL BY BUILDING TRUST

———

"Women, who are a majority of the peoples of the earth, are indispensable to the accumulation of the kind of social capital that is conducive to development, peace, justice, and civility."
—MAHNAZ AFKHAMI, WOMEN'S RIGHTS ACTIVIST, FOUNDER AND PRESIDENT OF WOMEN'S LEARNING PARTNERSHIP.

I was laughing so hard I had tears coming out of my eyes. I had wandered into the office kitchen looking for some sort of food or beverage pick-me-up to get me through the dragging Friday afternoon. I came across two of my female colleagues and we started chatting about the upcoming weekend.

The conversation turned to our kids, as it often does, and we ended our chance encounter in a fit of giggles. It was then that I realized that thanks to the COVID-19 pandemic, it had been eighteen months since I had this kind of uplifting, spontaneous kitchen conversation at work. And it felt great.

On the one hand I am fully aware of how privileged I am to have had—and to have kept—a job that allowed me to work from home during this past year and a half. I would be lying, however, if I said I hadn't missed the bonding that happens in spontaneous kitchen conversations, or in the shared misery of the 3 p.m. scavenger hunt for whatever caffeine/snack boost will get folks to the day's finish line, or in a coworker's "quick question" that turns into a thirty-minute conversation about the latest show on Netflix.

It is through these interactions, whether they are chance encounters, scheduled meetings, organized committee work, and the like, that help people build trust. Sometimes this trust helps us convert these relationships from cordial colleagues to, dare I say, lifelong friends.

In this chapter, we will explore how women and men build trust. Regardless of gender, trust is built using three main tools: sharing information, the way we use language, and through emotional intelligence. But it turns out that women use these tools differently than men, and it is that difference that is the key to understanding how women work.

Self-Disclosure

Information-sharing falls into two main categories: transparency and self-disclosure. When we talk about transparency, we generally mean leadership sharing information to front-line staff within an organization. This type of information sharing is important from an organizational perspective because employees are more likely to go along with decisions made by leadership if they understand the thinking behind them.

Teams who understand the *why* behind decisions tend to be more willing to move together toward a shared goal, whether that goal is the organization's mission or deciding what kind of coffee to order for the office (although I would argue that coffee type is almost as important as organizational mission, but I digress).

Self-disclosure, on the other hand, is more personal. It is exactly what it sounds like: disclosing—or sharing—information about oneself. When people self-disclose, they could be sharing information as trivial as what they had for breakfast or as deep and personal as a medical diagnosis.

During that kitchen conversation, my two colleagues and I weren't talking about anything particularly deep or personal. We were simply sharing some parenting insights we had stumbled across in being the mothers of boys. But that innocuous, spontaneous exchange of just a little bit of our personal lives built additional trust between myself and my colleagues. For women, specifically, self-disclosure allows us to see coworkers as whole people rather than just allies, adversaries, or people who happen to share the same too-hot/too-cold office space.

There is a significant amount of research dating back to the early 1970s that shows that disclosing personal—but not too personal—information leads to building trust among colleagues, particularly among women. In 1977, Lawrence Wheeless and Janis Grotz investigated the relationship between trust and self-disclosure. The findings were twofold:

first, when women self-disclosed, trust between the person sharing (the sharer) and the recipient of the information increased. Secondly, the *more* information disclosed, the higher the resulting level of trust.

For women, knowing someone on a more personal level makes us more patient and understanding with each other. When we know someone more holistically, we can pause and remember that perhaps there are external reasons for things going awry. Perhaps a project is late because the colleague is emotionally drained from caring for an ailing parent, not because they are unorganized. Perhaps a colleague snapped at a customer because of the lack of sleep a new baby brings. Or perhaps she didn't respond to that late night email because her pet was at the emergency vet's office. Self-disclosure can help lead to empathetic understanding and more patience with our colleagues.

At the other end of the spectrum, however, is oversharing. As Lynn Offerman and Lisa Rosh discuss in their *Harvard Business Review* article, "Building Trust Through Skillful Self-Disclosure," sharing without oversharing is a fine line for leaders. They mention that research points to increased trust of leaders by subordinates when leaders share personal information; however, sharing *too much* information or information that is simply too personal can backfire.

"Leaders have to walk a fine line when it comes to self-disclosure. Skillful self-disclosers choose the substance and process of their revelations, including the depth, breadth, and timing of disclosure, with the goal of furthering the collective task rather than furthering personal agendas. Too much disclosure might be met with revulsion, as in the case of a manager we worked with who joked about his sexual prowess using baking metaphors during a senior leadership retreat, to the horror of his listeners. Too little disclosure may result in follower feelings of uncertainty and suspicion, with followers unable to trust someone who isn't open about his or her own background" (Offermann and Rosh, 2012).

Additionally, sharing isn't something that comes naturally to everyone. In her book *The Likeability Trap*, Alicia Menendez cites a friend who was criticized at work for not sharing enough of her personal life and was encouraged to go to her boss for dating advice. At the same time, Menendez's friend Marisol had zero interest in sharing her life outside of work with her colleagues. "I don't want anyone to ask me what I did over the weekend, and I don't want to know what they did over the weekend," says the friend. Unfortunately for both women, there is an excellent chance that by not sharing even something as trivial as favorite TV shows, they will miss out on building essential social capital, which can hurt their careers in the long run (Eagly and Carli, 2007).

So friends, please, share away—with caution. If you are comfortable with talking about your kids, your pets, or your partners, then do so. It will go a long way to making your work environment more comfortable and to building social capital. But like any tool, self-disclosure can be overused, so do some self-reflection to know where to draw your own line about what to share about yourself and when.

Language

Of course, it's impossible to disclose any sort of information to someone else without using language. Comedians, actors, and men in general have made women's penchant for talking the butt of many a joke. But the fact of the matter is that women will often use different language—and more of it—when speaking with other women than when speaking with men, whether it is at home, work, or elsewhere. Catherine, a vice president at a tech firm whom I interviewed for this book, discovered this difference firsthand.

Catherine began her career in higher education, moving upwards within the university system before moving into tech. Because of her career trajectory, she had the unique experience of working in both a primarily female environment in higher education as well as a primarily male environment in tech. When I asked her about the differences between the two worlds, she mentioned things like the speed of decision making and using data as metrics, but the main difference she has noticed is the use of language.

In higher education, language was softer and more indirect, according to Catherine. Criticism, no matter how constructive, needed to be conveyed with greater delicacy and diplomacy. "In my current setting, I can edit a document and add a comment that simply says, 'Awkward sentence—reword,' without offending the author. There is no way I could be that direct in higher education," says Catherine. In higher ed, the request to rephrase would have to be buffered by additional context or comments that indicated support, encouragement, or at the very least, that the feedback wasn't personal.

I chuckled at this anecdote, as it reminded me of a "talking to" I had received when I first started in higher ed. In previous jobs and industries, email conversations were more like a tennis match. Responses to initial questions were often just a sentence or a phrase, or sometimes even just one or two words. The "Dear So-and-So" was often left off. I, and others in my previous work lives, jumped right into the meat of the conversation.

Not so in higher education.

Soon after I began my higher ed career, my supervisor came to me and asked me to watch my tone in my emails. I was too direct, and I needed to soften my language. I needed to use introductions, to be sure to *always* say thank you, and to sign my full name.

I felt a bit like a misbehaving child being corrected after that conversation. I wasn't intentionally being rude; I was just getting to my point, being efficient. But in the predominantly female world of higher education, it turned out that I needed to soften language, to include formal introductions and closings, and just more words to be liked by my colleagues.

Victoria Nash's 2018 research supports our experiences. She notes that societal expectations for gendered language are strong forces in the workplace. In her paper "Gendered Language: Women's Linguistics in the Workplace," she states that in our society, women are expected to act and speak in a more nurturing, emotional, and personal way, and are also expected to divulge more personal information (Ridgeway & Smith-Love, 1999).

In her literature review, Nash also found that women in a variety of female-dominated environments told lengthier stories and often ended thoughts with a question, demonstrating less security in their statements. She also noted that those women who were more direct and assertive in their language were quickly admonished by other women, sometimes being called a tyrant. Her review supported Ridgeway & Smith-Love's finding that women were expected to use language that was more nurturing, emotional, and softer.

However, when women use these more female language tactics in *male*-dominated environments, they pay a price. Women politicians in Ecuador's legislative congress were observed to be interrupted more often during their speeches on the legislative floor than the male politicians, particularly at lower ranks within the congress (Vallejo Vera and Gomez Vidal, 2020).

Women, particularly those who were new to the congress, were observed to use more words and give lengthier speeches. Unfortunately, they were then interrupted more, taking away valuable time and access to the legislative floor. Women quickly learned, then, to shorten their speeches and use fewer words to avoid being interrupted and maintain their access to floor time. In other words, the women legislators had adjusted their behavior to fit in with the men.

These studies show that women can run into a damned-if-you-do, damned-if-you-don't situation. Those women pursuing upward career trajectories find themselves having to make a choice: use softer and more language to fit in with women, or use more direct and less language to fit in with men.

There are some women, however, who have figured out how to do both at the same time, to adjust their language to their audience. These women tend to have high levels of awareness of the emotions of people around them and can adjust their behavior to match their audience. This skill is called emotional intelligence, and those women who have it and use it tend to do very well in their careers.

Emotional Intelligence

Emotional intelligence has become something of a buzzword in business education circles over the past decade or so. First coined in 1964, the concept gained popularity in leadership education since the 1990s thanks to the research conducted by Peter Salovey and John D. Mayer. In 2005, psychologist and thought leader Daniel Goleman wrote a book simply titled *Emotional Intelligence*, which became an international best seller and spawned many more books, articles, and classroom lectures on the topic.

Goleman describes emotional intelligence, or more simply EQ, as an ability to identify and regulate four components: empathy, self-awareness, social skills, and emotional management (*Psychology Today*, 2011). Self-awareness is simply being aware of one's current emotional state and behaviors, while managing our emotions means regulating appropriate reactions to stimuli in the environment. Empathy is being able to relate to and understand someone else's emotional state, while social skills dictate how to interact with others in culturally appropriate ways. While no one person has the perfect balance of all four parts, some have a better balance of the ingredients than others.

Ask the average person, given the definitions above, whether women have more emotional intelligence than men, and most people would say yes. But it's a bit more complicated than that, especially when it comes to the workplace and leadership. What Goleman found in his research is that while women generally tend to have more emotional intelligence than men, those differences diminish and even evaporate as you move up the corporate ladder and to the CEO/executive level of the top performing companies. He cites a study by HayGroup Boston that found that while women's emotional intelligence remained steady up and down the various corporate ladders studied, there was no statistically significant differences between men and women when it comes to emotional intelligence at the top. Those men at the top exhibited more emotional intelligence than those men at lower levels within the organizations.

So, what does this have to do with women at work? Emotional intelligence is one of women's superpowers and we should be using more of it at work. The old advice given to women—to act more like a man to compete with the men—is false if a woman wants to be at the executive level. But if we allow ourselves to rely on our natural emotional intelligence, then we should succeed and rise higher within various organizations the more often we use it.

Catherine, the ed tech executive introduced in the previous discussion on language, confirms this research. I asked Catherine about EQ in our interview for this book. I asked her if there would ever be a time, as a woman in a position of leadership, when she would be willing to spend some of her own social capital on another, more junior woman in her office. What would make her want to advocate for a woman below her on the ladder to move up in the organization? Her answer:

"I have a woman on my team who is particularly astute at managing up. She's learned my style and anticipates what I might need to best lead the team. Regularly, she asks, 'What can I do to make your job easier?' And to me, that is one of the most powerful questions someone can ask their leader. Yes, it's the leader's responsibility to help their team members grow, to challenge them, to support them. But what's been lost over the past few years is the idea that it's also your job to support your boss, no matter what level you are at. When someone can understand the pressures that are coming from above me, around me, and do what they can to help me and the team, as a whole, be successful, I will absolutely ensure she has a seat at the table. That level of leadership maturity indicates a

readiness to take on greater responsibility and navigate more complexity. I would not hesitate to elevate, recognize, and give this person the opportunity to shine. She has strong EQ and can read the room. Those who show me high levels of EQ are generally going to get my support."

Women who have this level of self-awareness of their own skills, can empathize with others, can interact in socially-appropriate ways, and can manage their own emotions in stressful situations are going to earn the trust of those above them and around them. It can be a tool that a woman can use to rise to the top, especially when she is focused on the mission as well as the good of the people working for and around her.

Where Do We Go from Here?

We've looked at the tools that women use to build trust to be successful in the workplace: self-disclosure, language, and emotional intelligence. And yes, someone who uses those tools sounds like the ideal person to work with.

What happens, though, when a woman uses one of those tools too often? What if she is an over-sharer or doesn't share enough information? What if she talks too much or can't read the room? Or doesn't use one of the tools mentioned? In those cases, she often emerges as a stereotype.

Too concerned with her own career and not focused on the needs of her team? *She might be a Control Freak.* Isn't aware of how her behavior affects others? *She might be a Queen Bee.* Isn't telling you why something needs to be done? *She might be The Quiet One.*

While many stereotypes have popped up in my research for this book, certain ones were mentioned more often than not. Throughout the remainder of this book, I've dedicated a chapter to each of the more common stereotypes. And not just to the negative stereotypes, but to some of the positive ones as well. Because as much as we should be aware and learn how to handle the Queen Bees and Control Freaks, we should also learn from the True Leaders how to become more confident in our own leadership styles. (Hint: it has a lot to do with EQ.)

In each chapter, you'll see a description of a stereotype, some research as to why your boss/colleague/subordinate falls into that stereotype, and how you might try to work with her.

Keep in mind, however, that the only behavior you can truly control is your own. While you might be able to come to a polite working environment with a Queen Bee, the likelihood of changing her behavior is slim to none. As a result, my advice to anyone is always look at yourself, look at your situation, and decide if staying there is the right move for you. Sometimes it is and sometimes it isn't, but only you can make that decision for yourself.

PART II

THE STEREOTYPES

—

CHAPTER 4

THE QUEEN BEE

"In every hive, there can only be one queen bee."
—QUOTE FROM A TOASTMASTERS PARTICIPANT LIVING
WITH HER MOTHER-IN-LAW IN TOKYO, JAPAN

I thought I had left behind the world of vicious female behavior at my college graduation. Little did I know at the time it would find me again in the working world just a few years later.

Carmen and I worked together as marketing managers for about a year. She had been at the company for many years before I arrived and had developed a reputation for doing good work and was well respected by her colleagues. During this particular summer, Carmen and I both reported to a woman named Jane.

Unfortunately for us, Jane was going through a divorce. And she was pissed.

Jane took her frustration out on everyone around her. She gossiped about subordinates to other managers right in front them. She accused Carmen of excluding her from projects and keeping her out of the loop; Carmen later received hundreds of "deleted without being read" email receipts and meeting invites for updates about said projects. The events in question were never particularly extreme, but when threaded together, they made for a very long summer for both of us.

Unfortunately, Jane's behavior is not unique. There are hundreds, if not thousands, of online articles offering advice to working women about how to deal with behavior described as bullying, toxic, nasty, mean. In today's psychological and sociological literature, this behavior is often referred to as Queen Bee behavior and in reading through the research, it describes Jane to a T. Carmen and I were fortunate to have each other as moral support that summer; it was the only way we both survived.

What Is a Queen Bee?

When I first began interviewing women about their experiences in working with other women, the response was always, "Oh my gosh, do I have a story for you." Everyone had a Queen Bee story, and it was THE story they wanted to tell first.

One of the women I interviewed was Paula, a CEO of her own environmental education firm. During our conversation, we talked a lot about how she works with many women in various aspects of her company and as clients. She describes most of her encounters as positive, but she unfortunately had a Queen Bee boss when she first started graduate school.

Paula had just started her academic program and had simultaneously started working at an internship. Like most graduate students, Paula worked part-time at her internship while spending most of her time on her studies. But her supervisor expected Paula to drop everything for her work. Paula was to attend meetings at any given time of day with little to no advance notice. Paula was expected to be at her boss's beck and call.

"She was constantly wanting me to come to these meetings with her during my class time. When I told her I couldn't because of class, she said, 'I don't understand why this is a choice.' Of course, I was paying to go to school to learn so my priority was going to class. When I tried to explain this to her, her response was, 'Well then, your priorities are upside down. Your priority should be me.'" Paula quit the internship shortly thereafter.

Paula's boss was demonstrating classic Queen Bee behavior: exhibiting destructive behavior toward other women in the interest of furthering her own career. Payscale.com defines a Queen Bee as "a woman who treats subordinates who are women more critically than she does male subordinates." We don't know if Paula's boss treated men in similarly subservient ways, but the good news for Paula was that she saw the early signs of Queen Bee behavior and was able to leave before it got worse.

Unfortunately, this behavior is not new in the workplace. While it may be fodder for reality TV and the movies—think *Mean Girls* or *Pretty in Pink*—in the workplace it can make life miserable. It is this misery that caught the attention and interest of psychologists in the US as early as the 1970s.

In 1974, Graham Staines, Toby Epstein Jayaratne, and Carol Tavris from the University of Michigan surveyed two hundred thousand women to determine whether they had been bullied in the workplace. They found that women who rose through the ranks in male-dominated environments were likely to oppose the rise of other women and would actively work to keep other women down. These executive women had worked to achieve their proximity to or place of power and saw that there wasn't room for other women at the top. To protect their own careers, they bullied others into staying where they were or into leaving the organization altogether.

With the women's equal rights movement of the 1970s and 1980s, and the sheer numbers of women entering the workforce in the 1990s, one would think the Queen Bees would have died off, especially as women moved into middle and upper management. But no, they are alive and well, according to Peggy Drexler, author of the 2013 *New York Times* article, "The Tyranny of the Queen Bee."

Drexler's article highlights Kelly, an up-and-comer at a consulting firm who had a run-in with a Queen Bee at work. While Kelly had gained the respect of coworkers and other partners, she unfortunately found herself being cut off by her female supervisor in meetings and excluded from conversations. She then discovered her boss was talking to other partners about moving Kelly to a different position that would be "more in-line with her skills." Her skills were just fine and, in fact, her work was well respected.

Drexler's research found these patterns to repeat over and over again. The women in her research assumed there is room at their current level or above for only one Queen, and that Queen should be her. The women in Drexler's study also actively worked to ensure that each was the only Queen in her hive; this is after forty additional years of women's empowerment and fights for equal rights at work and in society.

How Does One Become a Queen Bee?

In Western societies, women are expected to adhere to a certain set of behaviors. They are expected to be the caretakers, the nurturers, and the child bearers. At the same time, most work environments reward traditional male-leaning behavior, such as competitiveness, frankness, and prioritizing work above all else. As a result, women feel the pull of trying to live up to two sets of expectations: trying to be the gentle and caring woman while also trying to be aggressive in growing her career.

Research shows that Queen Bees evolve out of this juxtaposition. A literature review conducted in 2015 by Derks, Van Laar, and Ellemers posits that Queen Bee behavior is not necessarily innate to women, but rather a reaction to living and working in a male-dominated society while simultaneously being expected to display typical "female" behavior assigned to their gender.

The researchers reference an idea called Social Identity Theory (Tajfel and Turner, 1979), which states that people form their identity based on their gender, among several other factors. However, when the gender in question is in the minority and has restricted access to power and resources, members of that gender begin to attribute these restrictions to the behaviors of their group. Women, concerned that by identifying outwardly with other women who display such "female" behaviors, will then begin to do or more of the following:

- behave more like the dominant group in power, usually men;
- physically and psychologically distance themselves from other women, particularly junior women; and/or
- endorse and legitimize the current gender hierarchy.

For example, let's say Mary and I are friendly coworkers. She and I are one of the few women in our office. Mary and I are at work, and she breaks down crying in the kitchen, in view of men at higher levels of the office. I might feel embarrassed by Mary's show of emotion because crying is not necessarily acceptable within our office, particularly by the men. I assume the men in power don't want to work with a "crier" so I will view her "female" behavior as threatening to my career progress. To keep my career trajectory, I will begin distancing myself from Mary and/or start committing more of my time and self to my work, to align with values of the group in power—men. In summary, I have just elicited Queen Bee behavior.

Similarly, the Social Justification Theory we discussed in chapter two also saw subgroups of women trying to distance themselves from each other. The women in that study feared being lumped in with other groups of women who displayed more "female" behavior. Anxious this judgment could sociologically lead to a disruption in access to power, Queen Bee behaviors emerged.

This distancing response is more pronounced when senior women interact with junior women in the same organization. On top of seeing junior women display more "female" behavior, senior women view them as not having sacrificed enough in their lives to reach their same level. They haven't yet missed their children's soccer games, haven't yet missed as many of their partner's birthdays, or haven't yet missed as many hours with loved ones as the senior women have. And until they do, the junior women will be pushed away from upward opportunities by the senior women (Derks, Van Laar, and Ellemers, 2015).

Finally, I would argue that because our society as a whole is male dominated, much of this Queen Bee behavior is learned well before women enter the workforce. Anyone who has been to high school has seen Queen Bee behavior in action; it doesn't start in adulthood. This is why Queen Bee behavior is found in all-women work environments as well: women carry that learned behavior with them throughout their careers unless or until they feel the threat of potential group expulsion lessen or disappear.

When anyone feels insecure in a work environment for any reason, they will respond in their own way. Some will rise above, some will respond with people-pleasing behavior, while some will respond with quiet strategizing, as we will see in later chapters. Queen Bees happen to respond with the negative behavior associated with the stereotype: hostility, bullying, distancing from other women, and conforming to the behavior of those in power.

But knowing what we now know, we must look for opportunities to channel that negative energy into positive outcomes.

Queen Bee Strengths and Weaknesses

Queen Bee behavior is often the most difficult to deal with, which is why I discuss this stereotype first in this book. The dark side of Queen Bee behavior is a wide variety of bullying and passive aggressiveness, or just plain ol' aggressiveness. Queen Bee bosses may take credit for work you have done or accuse you of not doing the work you actually did. Queen Bee coworkers may spread rumors and gossip or leave out pertinent project information that may be a key to your project's success. Queen Bee subordinates may act glowingly around you while simultaneously going above your head without informing you of their intentions.

On the upside, when Queen Bee energy is channeled in the right direction or they are given the right incentives, Queen Bees get shit done. They feel like, or know, they are being watched, so they will often go above and beyond to make themselves look good. They are generally achievers, looking to add to their resume and check things off their list. They tend to network vertically and have "friends" in high places or strive to make friends in the right places. Recognizing their energy and what incentivizes them is key because while Queen Bees can be work horses, their behavior can turn sour on a dime and the outcome is often the destruction of relationships with and around them. Queen Bees need a lot of assurance that their job will be there for the long haul to lessen their overall anxiety.

How to Work with Queen Bees

In the literature review we discussed previously, Derks, Van Laar, and Ellemers also reference different ways to deal with Queen Bee behavior. At an organizational level, two practices can help Queen Bees improve their behavior: self-affirmation and positive feedback from supervisors. If there is enough awareness in the organization that Queen Bee behavior exists, then training in self-affirmations can be provided. When those in the minority group (in this discussion, women) are asked to focus on their own strengths and the strengths of other women, Queen Bees often begin to reintegrate or reduce their distance to the group. Additionally, when supervisors provide positive feedback to the Queen Bees, they become more confident in their work and within their workplace.

Of course, not all organizations, offices, units, or groups have that level of awareness. Nor do Queen Bees always want to change their behavior. This means you must figure out how to work with them as they are.

The good news is that when working for a Queen Bee boss, you may be able to ride her coattails to meet people she knows throughout the organization. Queen Bees tend to be good networkers, and she may be willing to introduce you to her contacts. Even if she isn't willing to introduce you, you can learn how to network vertically within your organization through observation. You can also learn a lot of the unwritten rules in your organization and what is valued by upper management by watching how the Queen Bee interacts with others. Her behavior can give great insight as to how to move up and how to use those unwritten rules to your own benefit.

If you are a manager and have a Queen Bee working for you, put her to work. Ask her what her career goals are (chances are she has them well-defined) and help channel her energy into projects that will help her feel confident and unthreatened. Give her her own hive—or project—that she can manage and let her figure out how to manage it, with well-defined guardrails in place. Queen Bees thrive off a challenge and the resulting outcome. Also, know that the Queen Bee may not stick around for very long, especially if she is ambitious, so having a contingency plan to replace her is wise.

And what if your coworker is a Queen Bee? As we discussed in chapter one, building trust is key in working relationships. Queen Bees, by nature, trust others very little. But it's worth a shot to build some trust to show that you are not a threat. Sometimes just a friendly conversation on noncontroversial topics will go a long way to calm the tension. Work with your supervisor(s) to establish boundaries on projects so you aren't overlapping in responsibilities, if possible. In short, give her space and let her take the lead in her own hive.

Sherri Staack, author of *Tune into WOW Leadership*, also advises women to take a cautious, individual approach to addressing Queen Bee behavior. Regardless of what your relationship is with the Queen Bee—boss, coworker, or subordinate—keep everything professional and documented by saving emails and keeping a journal of the comments that may not appear in documents. Then, if you do feel like you need to go to your manager or HR to report the behavior, compile the evidence, and position it as a business problem.

Staack quotes Dr. Gary Namie, cofounder and director of the *Workplace Bullying Institute*. "Report [the behavior] to your superiors and make it a business case on how the bully is affecting your productivity and driving up absenteeism. The minute you talk about how emotionally traumatized you are, you're unlikely to get any help."

However, these very adult and mature ways of dealing with problems don't always work. Without naming names, I have seen people in various types of organizations report bad behaviors to upper levels of management only to get pushed out themselves. Firing people is difficult in most organizations, damn-near impossible in others, particularly at high levels in organizations. In these instances, it's easier to get rid of the lower-level woman as she may be less costly to fire or push out. You may have to decide if the organization you work for is worth the fight. Sometimes it is, and sometimes it isn't.

Like any stereotype, there are positives and negatives. Queen Bees can backstab, sabotage, and gossip, but understanding they likely sacrificed a lot to get to where they are and likely feel threatened in their position can go a long way to understanding their mindset. Do your best to learn to get along—or at least work—with the Queen Bee but protect yourself as well: document everything and work with managers and HR if needed. In the end keep in mind you can only control your own behavior. If you've followed protocol, documented the bad behavior, have gone up the chain and things still have not improved, sometimes it's best for your own mental health to just move on.

CHAPTER 5

THE CONTROL FREAK

———

"Never mind—I'll just do it myself."
—ANY GIVEN WOMAN ON ANY GIVEN DAY.

I am a confessed control freak when it comes to laundry. I really don't care much about fashion, nor do I spend any sort of money on clothes. However, I'm *very* particular about scents and wrinkles so I have a structured system for washing and folding clothes.

In the spirit of personal development, however, I've recently tried to ease the control freak in me by delegating household tasks. Just recently, I attempted to teach my fourteen-year-old son how to fold his own shirts to spare myself a little bit of housework and to help him develop some basic life skills.

Let me say, the process was painful.

First, I showed him the easiest way to fold a shirt. Then I gave him a shirt and had him do it. While he attempted the various steps, I kept reaching over to move his hands to the right spot on the seams of the shoulders and then to help him smooth out the sleeves and other wrinkles before folding, until finally he said, "Mom, I'VE GOT IT." Then he said, laughing, "This is killing you, isn't it?" I tried to save a little bit of face with some comment along the lines of, "No, I'm just trying to show you how." But he knew that deep inside I was dying a slow, painful death while watching him fold that shirt.

The lesson ended after just that one shirt; I folded the rest.

While watching my son fold clothes was difficult for me, I also know firsthand that it can be equally as difficult, and sometimes downright demeaning, to work for and with others who are highly controlling. I've worked for women who have monitored and corrected my every move, which made me feel stupid and incompetent. Having had my own work corrected over and over again was exhausting at best and insulting at worst.

What has saved me and my self-esteem in these situations is the realization that a person's need for control is not about me specifically, but about her own fear and anxiety. Anxiety about not having the time to do everyone's job her own way and fear other's mistakes will reflect poorly on her. And while this realization didn't make the process of working for her any easier, it did help my own mental health.

What Is Control?

Because the word "freak" can be degrading, I'm going to refer to control freaks as Controllers from here on out. But either way, I put the Controller stereotype right after the Queen Bee stereotype because Controllers are almost as difficult to deal with. Perhaps not as vicious as Queen Bees, but they can still make your life miserable. I should know, as I've worked for many Controllers and, if I'm being honest, it is the stereotype I most closely identify with.

Before we discuss what a Controller is, we should first discuss the idea of control. According to the American Psychological Association, control is defined as "authority, power, or influence over events, behaviors, situations, or people." People who are mentally healthy tend to believe the choices they make when faced with a decision affect the outcome of that decision (Leotti, Iyengar, and Ochsner, 2010). As such, healthy people are more resilient in the face of difficult challenges. They believe they can make a difficult choice, and everything will work out. While they may be nervous about making such a choice, they have confidence that in the end they, as a human being, will be okay.

However, sometimes that resiliency diminishes for a variety of reasons. Some people no longer believe they will be okay in the face of difficult choices, so they try to control more variables to reduce their anxiety. For these folks, they begin to believe they are the *only* people who can make correct choices and if they aren't the ones to control all the details, the world around them will fall apart (Meyers, 2010).

Emma is a fellow higher education colleague of mine who worked for a Controller named Nancy. She started telling me anecdotes about Nancy's need for controlling a variety of details in their office that were way below Nancy's level of responsibility.

Their office had a lobby for students who were waiting for appointments with staff. For whatever reason, Nancy had the couches in the lobby set up so when students sat in them, they faced the wall. No one was sure why the couches were set up that way. The staff wondered if Nancy didn't realize that students were facing the wall when they sat on the couches. Maybe she wasn't concerned about the lobby and just didn't care about how the furniture was set up. Maybe Nancy would be happy to see another design that made more sense. When Nancy went out of town for a conference, the staff decided it would be a good time to rearrange the couches to make the space more comfortable and welcoming for students.

Nancy was NOT happy with this new arrangement. Upon her return to the office, she called the entire staff into a meeting and accused them of "attempted mutiny." Nancy then doubled down on her control efforts in other areas. Emma once printed a flyer listing academic requirements for a major on pink paper to display in their office lobby; Nancy made her throw those flyers out and reprint them on orange paper because "pink paper is too feminine; boys won't declare that major if it's printed on pink paper." She followed Emma around the building before large events straightening directional signs, insisting they were crooked when they weren't. She even went so far as to stop ordering pastries for weekly staff meetings because she felt staff members were "eating too many calories."

In short, Nancy exerted control over all aspects of how the office was run, particularly those details that seemed inconsequential to the student experience. Fortunately for Emma, both she and Nancy moved on to work at different universities, so we were able to chuckle about these ridiculous anecdotes.

But in our conversation, we started asking the question, "Why?" Why did Nancy care so much about the way the furniture was arranged, about the color of the paper, or what the staff members ate?

What we surmised is that Nancy was afraid. *Very* afraid. Afraid of what others at the university thought of her, afraid of how parents and visitors to the university might judge her, afraid she might be "found out." Emma wasn't sure what Nancy felt she needed to hide; she was never able to get to know her on any sort of personal level. But Nancy's anxiety and fear led her to try to control every single detail of everything around her, only to make everyone around her miserable.

How One Becomes a Controller

It turns out humans have a biological and psychological need for control. In a 2010 literature review called "Born to Choose: The Origins and Value of the Need for Control," authors Leotti, Iyengar, and Ochsner explain that all voluntary human behavior is determined by choice. Some choices are big, like what company to work at and whom to marry, while others are small like whether to take a sip of water. But this awareness of choice leads humans to believe we can exert some control over our surrounding environment, and therefore exert some control over the outcomes of our decisions.

There is some evidence that this need for control is inborn. Research has shown that once children master a skill, such as feeding themselves, they become resistant to adult attempts to influence or control this ability (Kochanska and Aksan, 2004). Anyone who has spent any amount of time with preschoolers trying to dress themselves has seen this need for control in action.

As we carry this need for control in adulthood, the potential loss of control can present as fear. Fear of being found out as a fraud (impostor syndrome), fear of not being liked, fear of not being trusted, and fear of losing social capital are just a few reasons given by psychologists regarding the roots of the need for control. As Seth Meyers, PsyD, points out in a 2016 *Psychology Today* article, "These people need control because, without it, they fear things would spiral out of control and their lives would fall apart."

For some people, the fear of a loss of control goes so far as to spiral into true psychological disorders, including obsessive-compulsive disorder, eating disorders, and other personality disorders. Whatever the cause, the fear of a loss of control very often presents itself as anxiety. "People who have control issues experience a lot of anxiety. They try to control things to reduce their anxiety level," says Dr. Susan Albers, PsyD, of the Cleveland Clinic.

So what does all of this mean for the Controller at work? Controllers are likely compensating for some sort of loss of control, or lack of choice, either at work or in another part of her life. It could be that she has a sick family member whose illness she can't fix. Or she can't please her own boss, so her solution is to take it out on you. Or she can't control her volume of work coming so she tries to control your work.

I would add based on the research I conducted about trust and social capital, women at work who have a high need for control also have very little trust for anyone else. They worry that if they are being judged based on someone else's performance, then any mistake made by that someone will reflect poorly on them, whether that other person is a subordinate, a teammate, or even a supervisor. In turn, whether consciously or unconsciously, she fears that someone else's mistake will result in her own decreased social capital. Controllers often feel they are constantly asked to prove themselves, over and over again.

Controller Strengths and Weaknesses

Like Queen Bees, Controllers by nature are generally achievers. Controlling for all aspects of projects, others' behavior, and for their own image has allowed them to experience some sort of success. Just like anyone with any sort of ingrained behavior, they repeat what has worked for them in the past. And the higher up a Controller gets, the more eyes she has on her, and the more controlling she may become.

If you are working for or with a Controller, the good news is that there is the potential for her success to reflect positively on you. Those Controllers who have the wherewithal to know their success took a village will give credit where credit is due. Controllers, particularly those higher up in an organization, are generally well respected by outsiders, and that respect can carry over to the team behind her.

While I don't recommend imitating her methods, you might be able to ride that wave of respect into different projects around your organization. At the very least, working with others in your organization outside of your department can be a distraction, some relief from the scrutiny you face day-to-day. At best it will help you network your way into another role within your organization, away from the Controller.

However, for every positive in working with a Controller, there are many negatives. Controllers will question your work, which in turn will make you question your own work. Controllers may even come behind you without your knowledge and "correct" your work. They may push you off projects, believing it's just easier and faster to do it themselves. In that case, any social capital you could have earned is no longer available to you. In the end you can become depressed, frustrated, and just plain bitter.

How to Work with a Controller

Les Parrott III, PhD, is the author of *The Control Freak* and recommends a few ways to handle the situation. The first is to take a breath and realize it's not about you. Just like the Queen Bee, you may be the recipient of the anxiety and control, but whatever the Controller's deep-down fear is, you didn't cause it. Once you have accepted this fact, Parrott recommends:

- **A little bit of empathy.** Consider what the Controller's anxiety might be related to. Is she trying to move up the ladder and is concerned about what higher ups might think? Has she broken the trust of those around her, either through her own doing or someone else's, and is afraid of losing her job? Parrott says that trying to look at things from the Controller's perspective can give you insight as to what is driving her behavior and can help you develop some empathy. It certainly won't solve the problem, but it might give you some peace of mind.
- **Understanding the "why" behind the way things are done.** Some Controllers like to do things a certain way because they've always been done that way. Controllers often fear the "new" because they aren't sure what the consequences will be when something new is tried. This is true particularly at large, older organizations. They revert to the way things are done out of comfort. But if you have a burning desire to try things in a new way, first understand why things are done the old way and be prepared to provide *lots* of potential benefits as to why a new way might be better.

- **Proposing a different strategy.** Parrott relays a story of Judy, a newspaper reporter who had a boss who wanted a run-down of every story she did as she was doing it. Judy found it was wasting a lot of time, so while it took a lot of courage, she asked him—politely—if she could simply provide a summary at the end of each story instead of running progress reports. The manager agreed and was quite relieved. So, if you know what is triggering your boss's or coworker's anxiety, you can recommend a way that would work for both of you, go for it.
- **Overwhelming the Controller with information.** Parrott gives his own example, and I can attest to the fact that this is a method that has worked for me. I once worked for a Controller whose biggest fear was of her own boss asking her a question for which she did not have an answer. Whenever I was working on a project for her, I always provided a myriad of reasons regarding any recommendations I made no matter how minute the detail, always highlighting the benefits *to her* of recommendations. The sheer amount of information I provided eventually helped her develop a trust that I could do the job. Fortunately, as time went on, I didn't have to provide as much information up front, although I always made sure I had it at the ready, just in case. Information is often an anecdote for a Controller's anxiety.

Finally, my own recommendation is to provide data about your success. One Controller I worked with responded well to data in the form of numbers and positive qualitative feedback. As we went through our time together, I collected data about the outcomes of various projects as well as any kind comments that came from our customers. I presented these at our weekly meetings and eventually she learned to trust the work that we as a team were doing.

In the end, as with all the difficult stereotypes, anything you can do to help your Controller build trust in you and your work is going to help ease the day-to-day working environment. But I end this chapter and every stereotype-focused chapter in this book with this thought: in the end, you can only control your own behavior. You may be able to earn her trust, or you may not. You might have to make a decision about whether to stay or whether to go.

CHAPTER 6

THE AMBITIOUS WOMAN

"We teach girls to shrink themselves, to make themselves smaller. We say to girls, 'You can have ambition, but not too much.'"

—CHIMAMANDA NGOZI ADICHIE, 2017 TED TALK

A former employee of my office was always described as "very... ambitious." And it was always said in hushed tones as if I wasn't supposed to know she was ambitious. She—who will remain nameless—had worked in my office several years before I started but we traveled in similar circles. I noticed for her, moving up in her career meant moving out of her current university to a new one. Higher education is a small world, so anytime her name came up, regardless of who I was talking to and which university they were from, she would always be described with the same hushed tones, "She was [pause] … ambitious."

It didn't seem to be an insult, but I could tell it wasn't a compliment either. When I pressed for more details as to why and how she was so ambitious, no one could really provide more. Was she being judged by people at each university for not staying there longer? Was it that she had the audacity to want to move up in the world? What's interesting is that I have since met her in person, and I, too, would describe her in the same way... ambitious. Very focused on the success of her organization, focused on growing her career, and on advocating for herself. But is that so bad?

What Is an Ambitious Woman?

In today's corporate lexicon, saying a woman is "ambitious" is often code for calling her a bitch. Those who call women "ambitious" seem to be of the opinion that these women are linearly and singularly focused on their own personal career goals at the expense of those around them. They will alienate others and destroy all relationships for the sake of power, status, and money.

However, I would argue that we are confusing Ambitious Women with Queen Bees. Truly Ambitious Women can indeed be successful and goal-oriented while at the same time caring, people-focused, and compassionate. Indra Nooyi, former CEO of PepsiCo, is a good example of someone who found that balance.

Originally from India, Indra Nooyi earned her bachelor's degree from Madras Christian College in 1976 and an MBA from the Indian Institute of Management. She came to the US and earned another master's degree in public and private management from Yale in 1980. Nooyi went on to marry, have two daughters, and joined PepsiCo in 1994, where she worked her way up to become the company's first female CEO in 2006. Since then, she has been granted numerous honorary doctorate degrees, is on the board of several Fortune 500 companies, and even had her portrait inducted into the Smithsonian National Portrait Gallery in 2019 (Nooyi, 2021).

And while profits more than doubled during her tenure at PepsiCo, achievement enough for any CEO, it was her focus on the people in the firm that pushed her to rock-star status. In 2006, she began doing something atypical of the average CEO: she wrote letters to the parents of her senior executives, thanking them for "the gift of their child to PepsiCo."

It sounds strange at first, but Nooyi was inspired by her experience returning to India after being named CEO at Pepsi. Her mother invited people over to the house to celebrate Indra's return home. But as the stream of visitors entered, Nooyi watched them congratulate *her mother* on her success, not Indra. She was hurt; after all, she was the one who had put in the work to climb the corporate ladder. But she soon realized her parents were the ones who had given her the tools to succeed; she simply used those tools to build her career.

So, upon her return to the US, she began building a people-focused culture at PepsiCo. Her mantra became purpose, performance, and people (Freeland, 2020). She wrote letters of thanks to her senior executive's families, acknowledging not only their hard work but the sacrifice that families made for those employees to spend time at the office. She worked to make PepsiCo a place not just for employees but for families, earning her an approval rating that consistently hovered around 75 percent (Ward, 2017).

What I love about this story is that Nooyi is a shining example of someone who is ambitious in today's world: focused on the profits while also caring for the people around her. She didn't feel the need to belittle her employees in an effort to streamline revenues; she didn't have to stomp on those around her to satisfy her own ego. She was able to be a successful CEO while also caring for others.

While Indra Nooyi exemplifies the Ambitious Woman, many other people have a hard time walking the very, very fine line between ambition and Queen Bee behavior. A person who is purely ambitious is defined someone "having a desire to be successful, powerful, or famous; or having a desire to achieve a particular goal" (Merriam-Webster, 2021). There is nothing in that definition about being hurtful or deceptive, but women who desire success, power, or fame also tend to be viewed as coldhearted and ruthless.

The most common and recent examples of those who have been accused of being "ambitious" are women who have recently run for president including Hillary Clinton, Elizabeth Warren, and Kamala Harris. They set their sights high and checked all the boxes along the way to run for president. Each had gone to college, to law school, and worked their way to the Senate before setting their sights on the highest office in the land.

Exactly like so many other men who have also run for president.

And while the male candidates who have run for office in recent memory have been applauded for their ambition, Clinton, Warren, and Harris have all been called nasty, shrill, and disloyal, respectively, in the same breath as being called ambitious.

Negative connotations of ambition are not limited to high profile people. A poll conducted by *Business Insider* in 2020 surveyed three thousand women and asked them whether having ambition is an important trait and whether they considered themselves ambitious. 59 percent of the women agreed that having ambition is important while 50 percent considered themselves ambitious. However, just 33 percent of the women would actually use the word ambitious to describe themselves, because of the poor reputation associated with ambitious women (Ward, 2021).

Additionally, research shows that women considered ambitious are less liked by their peers and supervisors (Riley Bowles, Babcock, and Lai, 2006), and are less likely to earn promotions (Snyder, 2014).

In thinking back to my own experience in trying to negotiate my salary, I wonder if I had been considered "too ambitious." As I mentioned, I had received a job offer, but when I attempted to negotiate the salary the offer was rescinded. I thought I was doing what women all over the world have been told to do: speak up for myself and advocate for what I was worth. But in that one question, "Could we possibly look at a higher salary?" Was I already being considered too ambitious, too aggressive, or too outspoken, even before I set foot in the door?

Like so many other women, upon receipt of that job offer, I adjusted my own behavior to seem nicer, more polite, and more appreciative. And I stayed that way for several years for fear of losing the job I had finally landed.

The good news is that today, ambition exists on a spectrum. In researching this book, I interviewed Lindy, a lifelong Air Force Airman—all members of the Air Force are called Airmen, regardless of gender; I checked. When I interviewed her, I asked her about her experience with women throughout her thirty-plus-year career. She had a wealth of experience and examples to share, including an experience with a colonel named Michelle.

Michelle was Lindy's boss and could be described as ambitious. But "she was at the opposite end of the ambition spectrum," says Lindy. "I mean still hard charging, but when you're in her presence, everything just slows down to a kind of elegance. There is just something about her and her style that calms and slows you down."

Lindy and Michelle were part of a team assigned to come up with a cohesive plan on how to recruit and retain talent across the four branches of the armed services, which are the Air Force, Army, Navy, and Marines. As the deadline approached, Lindy had done the necessary research but just couldn't meld all the commonalities and couldn't wrap her mind around how to prepare for the presentation. She had nothing ready to present, and the presentation was scheduled for the next day.

In a panic, Lindy decided to go to Michelle. "I needed her calm," said Lindy. "I knew she had her own part to get ready for because we were all in the hot seat. But she sat me down and took out a piece of paper and said, 'Tell me three things you want to get across at tomorrow's presentation.' She took just twenty minutes and helped me map out my thoughts. Then she said, 'You've done the work already; you just haven't put it together.' I will never forget that. So, when I think of ambitious women, I try to put them in the context of Michelle. Because she is ambitious and calm at the same time."

Lindy also described the other women on this team of five as ambitious, but each in their own way. Michelle was the calm one, while Kathy, another colonel, was a bulldog. She tended to steamroll over people to get the job done but still cared for those on her team. Mo was the cheerleader. If the team was doing a physical training test, Mo would be the one to drag the last person across the finish line. She could multitask all day while organizing a party for that night. Lindy once told Mo, "I can't even follow you on Instagram— it's too exhausting!"

While all these women exhibited different flavors of ambition, the one thing they all had in common was a focus on a goal with an intent to make *the team* successful. Whether that goal was delivering a presentation or passing a PT test, each of these women knew what the goal was and worked together to get it done.

They each had their own style but, regardless of *how* they did it, they focused on the mission without berating, backstabbing, or other negative behavior women are often accused of. And that is what really separates women—and men—who are ambitious from those who might veer into the Queen Bee category: being able to lead a team toward a goal while keeping in mind that each person on the team is an actual whole person and not just a cog in the wheel.

Strengths and Weaknesses of Ambitious Women

The great thing about truly ambitious women, like Indra Nooyi and Lindy's boss Michelle, is how much you can learn from them. Ambitious Women often have a lot of energy but have figured out how to focus that energy on moving a team toward a single goal. Truly ambitious women know how to juggle various parts of their lives and make it look easy, because they know how to delegate without dumping responsibilities on to others. And finally, many ambitious women will sweep others up in their own success and bring them along for the ride.

If the Ambitious Woman in your life has found this balance, learn from her! Just like in Lindy's example, there are many ways for women to be ambitious. You can be the bulldog, but you can also be the calm one or the cheerleader. Embrace your own style and embrace the people and their styles around you.

However, sometimes it's not all rainbows and unicorns when working with Ambitious Women. Ambitious Women like to be busy, which often makes their work environments busy places. She may not understand, or may forget, that others don't run at her pace, leaving you to feel overwhelmed. Additionally, Ambitious Women sometimes are so focused on their own career goals or their team's goals that they burn out. And it's often at this time that the Queen Bee or Controller behaviors emerge, driven by a fear of failing to get to the next career step or to achieve the next team goal.

How to Work with Ambitious Women

In the spectrum of the "Get me out the hell of here" (The Queen Bee—chapter four) to "I will always want to work for her" (The True Leader—chapter eleven), I would put the Ambitious Woman somewhere in the middle. The Ambitious Woman who knows how to harness her energy and direct it toward a mission can make a huge, positive difference in the organization and the lives of those around her. But leave that energy unchecked and she can sometimes turn into a bull in a china shop or veer off into Queen Bee territory. Understanding what motivates her and what her overall goals are can go a long way to making your life better in a work environment.

Ambitious women often thrive on goals, formulating plans to reach those goals, and reminding everyone what they should be doing to assist. Help her with those plans. Try to get her to focus on what the goal is and what the minimum steps are to accomplish that goal, just like Lindy's colonel did for her. Communicate to her that you are here to help and use your own style to try to assure her that it's going to be okay.

If the ambition starts to migrate into Queen Bee behavior, she is likely stressed. An honest conversation about what is bothering her and how you can help might be just what the doctor ordered. The simple question, "What help can I provide?" is sometimes enough to bring the Ambitious Woman's anxiety down. Ambitious Women also tend to take on a lot of work, so she will likely appreciate any support you can provide.

If bad behavior persists, however, you may have to bring in the experts: senior managers or HR. Documentation of bad behavior is key, and framing that bad behavior in a business context is also very helpful (e.g., we have lost three customers this week alone because Mary is yelling at them on the phone). Don't make it about you, unless the bad behavior is directed at you, in which case senior managers or HR should absolutely be involved.

And, as always, while it is easier said than done, you may have to make a decision as to whether to stay or go. If the "ambition" is adding on to your workload to the extent that it is too much, or the bad behavior is affecting you mentally or emotionally, and senior management/HR is of no help, you might have to look elsewhere. Yes, this may be difficult, but no job is worth your mental health.

CHAPTER 7

THE PEOPLE PLEASER

—

"Don't live your life to please other people."
—OPRAH WINFREY

It took cancer to break Sheryl Crow's habit of prioritizing everyone else in her life before her.

Born to a piano teacher and trumpet player in Missouri in 1962, Sheryl Crow was destined for music. She grew up listening to Elvis on the radio and went to college to become a music teacher. While she taught during the week, she spent her weekends singing and playing in bands and eventually recorded her first album *Tuesday Night Music Club*. This led to a stream of number one hits, additional albums, sixteen industry awards, movie parts, and so on (imdb.com, 2021).

Life took a turn, however, in 2006 when Crow was diagnosed with breast cancer. It was this life event that forced her to slow down and reevaluate her life. She told Tony Clayton-Lea of *The Irish Times* in 2014, "The cancer experience was a game-changer for me, and it also rebooted the way I looked at my life." As part of this reboot, Crow reflected on how she interacted with others. "I think I mastered the art of being a people pleaser," she says. "I found that I rarely said no to anyone, and I always made sure that everyone's needs were taken care of before my own."

As a result of her diagnosis Crow began to say no. "Every morning, as I lay on the radiation table, I faced the fact that I am the only person who can take care of me and that unless I take care of myself, I am no good to anyone else, including my children. I had to learn to say no to things I didn't want to do, even if it meant disappointing people."

Many women can relate to Crow's experience of being a People Pleaser. From the time we are children, women are taught to be accommodating, to please others, to always say yes even when we are exhausted, overcommitted, and stretched too thin in every part of life.

And often, it is this people-pleasing behavior that helps us succeed. Women who have risen through the ranks of their organization often did not get there by saying no. One wonders if Sheryl Crow's career success would have been the same had she said no more often. Like Crow, however, many women find that if they say no, it's not just the next door that closes, but many more doors beyond that one.

The Disease to Please

The phrase "the disease to please" was popularized by Dr. Harriet Braiker, a clinical psychologist who wrote extensively in the 1980s through the early 2000s about women's need to please. In her Oprah-famous book *The Disease to Please*, Braiker defines the "disease" as "the uncontrollable need for the approval of others." She goes on to say that people with the disease-to-please have debilitating fears of anger and confrontation, which force them to use niceness and people-pleasing as self-defense mechanisms.

Other psychologists more broadly define the "disease" as the need to belong. There is safety in numbers and the way to stay a part of a group, whether it is an ancient tribe from thousands of years ago or a modern-day, multinational corporation, is to make sure that those around us are happy with us and our performance. In our ancient tribes, we made others happy by sharing food, shelter, or through general camaraderie. Upsetting our fellow group members could have dire consequences such as being expelled from the group, leading to decreased access to food, shelter, and socialization (Abrams, 2017).

Fortunately, in today's world, being expelled from our social group or fired from our employer usually does not mean death. Saying no is more of an option in today's modern society, but for women it has little upside. At best, saying no to a boss could mean that future requests for better projects go to someone else. At worst, saying no can deplete her social capital, indicating that she is not a team player or not interested in participating in the group. For female bosses, saying no to a subordinate's request risks being labeled a tyrant. For female colleagues, saying no to other colleagues could indicate she is unfriendly, antisocial, or uncooperative, all of which go against society's expectations of women's behavior.

So what's a woman to do when she wants to be liked *and* to further her career? She says *yes*. Yes to projects within and outside her wheelhouse. Yes to being on committees and yes to being Snack Mom for the weekend's soccer game.

Yes to driving her parents to the doctor and to taking her pet to the vet.

Yes. To. Everything.

How One Becomes a People Pleaser

Women tend to fall into the trap of people-pleasing more so than men. One study surveyed over four hundred thousand adults between 2004 and 2008 to find that 54 percent of women were people pleasers as compared to just 40 percent of men (Kushner and Choi, 2010).

Colleen Long, PsyD, says our need to please usually starts in childhood. "We do something that pleases others, we get positive reinforcement—and we're hooked!" Little girls, in particular, are conditioned to please others.

As girls become teenagers and then young adults entering the working world, the advice given to them is to say yes to everything. Join clubs as a student! Ask for additional projects as an intern! Raise your hand for committees as a new hire! Saying yes allows the young worker to earn the trust of the supervisor and the colleagues that we've talked so much about in chapter two. Trust builds social capital and women can then move up the ladder from entry level to something higher. But somewhere along our rise to the top, we get bogged down in saying yes too often, and we become the People Pleaser.

It is sometimes hard to distinguish a Controller as defined in chapter five and a People Pleaser. As Sally Helgesen and Marshal Goldsmith explain in their book *How Women Rise*, "Like perfectionists, chronic people pleasers usually have difficulty delegating. Perfectionists resist it because they believe they can do everything better, while people pleasers are motivated by the desire to be helpful and a reluctance to burden others or let down anyone who might have relied on them in the past."

Lindy is the retired Air Force Airman we met when we talked about Ambitious Women in chapter six. In addition to our conversation about the different ways ambition expresses itself, she also mentioned she had a People Pleaser as a boss at one point in her career.

Lindy describes the situation as sad, because despite her colonel's many degrees and high levels of intelligence, she saw how others would take advantage of her need to please. When colleagues wanted something done, they didn't want to do themselves, they passed it off to the colonel, knowing she would always say yes and do it for them. "We couldn't leverage her talent very well because she was just like a pinball being batted around," says Lindy.

Lindy also felt frustrated because she saw herself reflected in the People Pleaser. "It made me really look at myself for all the times that I've set aside what I needed to do in order to make somebody else happy and then suffered later for it. And I get mad at myself, 'Why did I do that? Why couldn't I just tell them, no, maybe not now.'"

People Pleaser Strengths and Weaknesses

The strengths of People Pleasers are numerous. They are up for anything, obviously! They will say yes to lunch, yes to happy hours, yes to being a part of the team. They are usually happy-go-lucky and because they conform to the norms of womanhood, they are generally chatty, hardworking, and fun to be around.

From a work perspective, People Pleasers often develop a variety of skills and abilities because they say yes to everything. They've learned to adapt quickly and to multitask. And most often, they will get the work done. How can they not? They must please everyone around them.

But, as many of us reading this chapter know, saying yes has consequences for people other than People Pleasers. People Pleasers will agree with the boss and say yes to new projects, but when she can't get her own work done, she will turn to her colleagues and subordinates to ask for help, expecting them to say yes as well.

Cassandra is a friend of mine who works in publishing. Her people-pleasing boss's biggest fear was to have someone mad at her. She didn't want to rock the boat and wanted everyone to like her. So, she said yes to everything all the time. However, no one can do everything all the time, so the work fell to Cassandra's team. The team was being bombarded with one project and request after another, even before the most recent request was completed. It made for a chaotic work environment which in turn increased turnover. In her attempt to please everyone from outside the department, Cassandra's boss upset everyone inside her department, pleasing no one in the end.

Being a People Pleaser myself, and having worked for and with several others, I can attest to the fact that People Pleasers are happy until they are not. Once she has committed and overcommitted to those around her, her mental and physical health suffers. She becomes tired, stressed about not making all the deadlines she has committed to. She knows it's her fault for saying yes to so many things and then gets frustrated because there is no one to blame but herself. She might get so stressed that physical illness sets in, in which case even more people have to step in to help.

How to Work with a People Pleaser

Once you do a little armchair psychiatry, you can try to work around the People Pleaser's need to please. But first you need to figure out where her need to please is coming from. Questions to ask yourself about her behavior could include:

- Is she afraid of being fired so she says yes to everything?
- Is she avoiding conflict?
- Is she afraid it might be discovered that she can't do something or can't handle her job (impostor syndrome)?
- Is she anxious to move up in the organization, so she is hyper-focused on pleasing her own boss or those higher than her?
- Is she bored and saying yes to new things because they sound more fun than what she is doing now?

Ask About Priorities
Whether she is afraid of being fired, suffers from impostor syndrome, or is avoiding conflict, it's very likely her people-pleasing behavior is rooted in fear. I once worked for a woman who was terrified of others' opinions of her, of being "found out" that she might not belong in that high of a position. So, she said yes to any request from the outside and then handed off those new ideas to me and my colleagues. Of

course, this hand-off was then followed by some Controller behavior. It was not fun.

When I would get overwhelmed and couldn't keep up with her commitment of my time to others, I would ask her for her opinion on priorities, in writing. "Among the other things on my plate, where does this rank in priority?" Of course, the new thing was always the priority, but at least it was some level of permission to let go of a few things on my plate. Because she said yes to so many new requests, older projects were often no longer of interest. But it helped to remind her of the big picture, and she was happy to be consulted on what the priorities were.

If She Likes New Ideas...
If your boss is bored, then every new idea they come up with feels like a new fun thing to do. Elizabeth Grace Saunders, author of her 2018 article "How to Work with A Boss Who Has a New Idea Every Five Minutes," recommends you create a parking lot document that includes all the projects and tasks your boss has agreed to. Then, in a one-on-one meeting, you can go over all the items on the parking lot to see which ones she is still interested in. "Oftentimes your boss just wants to share something that's on her mind and is satisfied with acknowledgment of the idea," says Saunders. "The general rule in these situations is that you wait until the idea is brought up a few more times before doing anything, otherwise you can just let it sit."

Saunders also recommends giving a time estimate of the project back to the supervisor and asking where the new idea fits in with the mission and scope of your organization. Sometimes the reality of what it would take to implement something she has said yes to deflates the situation and it is no longer a priority. Or other times if she can't explain the connection between the idea and the mission, it again loses its luster.

Regardless of why the person is succumbing to people-pleasing behavior, the key is to use gentle, fact-based communication to remind the People Pleaser that there are only forty hours in a work week. She may end up working eighty hours per week herself, but that is her choice.

If she is repeatedly asking you to work extra hours to satisfy her own anxiety, then it's up to you to set your own boundaries. You are in your right to say no, but I recommend you explain why. And document those reasons. If needed, take the documented conversations to her manager or to HR and ask what the best next steps are. And of course, you may have to decide if it's worth staying around to work with or for her. After all, you are always in control of your own career; it might be worth moving on if her anxiety is too much for your own mental and physical health.

CHAPTER 8

THE AUTHENTIC WOMAN LEADER

———

"Sometimes people use who they are as an excuse. I know this guy, who would say something aggressive, and he's like, 'I know, I'm just an asshole. It's who I am.' And I'm like, 'Huh, you can change that, ya know?'"

—SIMON SINEK, CREATOR INSTITUTE

SPEAKER SERIES, MAY 2021

Pop Quiz:

Which one of the following is the definition of an Authentic Woman Leader?

1. Someone who pursues their passion, practices their values, connects with others, demonstrates self-discipline, and leads with their hearts *and* heads.
2. Someone who is locked into a rigid view of one's leadership, is rude and insensitive, refuses to change, will not adapt their leadership style to the circumstances.
3. All of the above.

The answer to this question *should* be A. When we think of Authentic Woman Leaders, we prefer to think of those who have high levels of emotional intelligence, own their mistakes, are focused on mission, and embrace the humanness of those they lead.

However, some leaders are authentically themselves but are also just jerks. They say they are "authentic" while insulting people around them, treating others poorly, and are focused more on their own self-serving goals rather than the goals of the team or the organization. "I am who I am—take it or leave it." They may not know they are offending everyone around them or may not care.

Which is why I classify the Authentic Woman Leader as a cautionary stereotype. Authentic Women might be living and working authentically, but also might also be very difficult to work with.

What Is an Authentic Woman Leader?

When asked to think of someone who is well-known for living an authentic life, Oprah Winfrey comes to mind. The "Queen of All Media" came from humble beginnings in Mississippi before going to college in Tennessee and landing her first gig on the 1980's Baltimore, Maryland TV show called *People Are Talking*. It was on this show that she discovered her niche and eventually went on to launch *The Oprah Winfrey Show* (Chan, 2021).

At the time of her eponymous show's launch, Oprah was doing what other, more famous talk show hosts at the time were doing: delivering tabloid entertainment on TV. It was when she hosted a panel of white supremacist skinheads that she decided she'd had enough. Oprah realized that she was giving the skinheads a platform to validate their beliefs rather than expose them for who they were. Right there and then, she decided that never again would she allow someone to use her platform for hate (OWN, 2015).

From there on out, Oprah decided to do her show her way. She talked about her own story, her own experiences with poverty and sexual abuse. She began demonstrating care and empathy for the guests she had on her show. She started being authentically herself as a host and as a celebrity. From there on out, her ratings soared, and she began building her multi-media empire. The rest, as they say, is history.

Oprah credits much of her success to her own authenticity. She stopped trying to follow the talk show crowd trends at the time and did what felt natural to her. She began living and working in a way that Bill George, professor at Harvard Business School and author of *Authentic Leadership*, defines as leading authentically. His definition of authentic leadership is answer A in the earlier pop quiz. It is someone who:

- Pursues her purpose with passion
- Practices solid values
- Establishes connected relationships with those she leads
- Demonstrates self-discipline
- Leads with her heart as well as her head

Oprah is, of course, a great example of someone who lives and leads authentically. But what happens if authenticity goes awry and you are dealing with someone who is a little *too* authentic? After all, history is full of political dictators who lived "authentically" while destroying the lives of millions of people around them.

Bullet point number five, "Leading with your heart as well as your head," is key in separating Authentic Women leaders from authentic jerks. Authentic Women take the time to consider how their actions impact those around them. Additionally, they are aware of their follower's needs and are willing to adjust their behavior to meet those needs.

Herminia Ibarra, PhD, is a professor at the London School of Economics and author of two books on the topic of authentic leadership. She also gave a TED Talk in which she discussed how she had to reexamine her interaction with others on her own journey to becoming an authentic leader in the classroom.

Dr. Ibarra tells the story of when she first started teaching in business school. She looked at her job as delivering information to her students. As such, she would stay up all hours of the night researching her topics and refining her presentations. Despite her best efforts, she consistently ranked at the bottom when it came to professor evaluations. Was she being true to who she was? Absolutely. Did her students respect her and look to her as a leader? Absolutely not.

Several colleagues tried to help her by giving her advice such as, "Just be yourself!" But ultimately, that was the problem—she was being herself. "Loads of people tried to help me," Dr. Ibarra said. "But as far as I could see, that was the problem.

I was too much myself—too introverted, too academic, too theoretical, too inexperienced, too scared."

She knew what her strengths and weaknesses were, and she could articulate them, but she didn't have the wherewithal to make adjustments to her behavior. She then took the advice of a colleague who encouraged her to look at the classroom as her own arena. Walk around, get to know the students, engage with them as people. And while she admitted that she would prefer to stay up all night, she knew she had to change.

So change she did. She began walking through the room as she lectured and interacted with her students. At first, it was strange to her and to them; after all, she had never entered their space before. But through these interactions, she discovered what her students were really interested in learning and could adjust from there, making for a more comfortable experience for everyone involved.

Dr. Ibarra learned that yes, authentic leaders are true to who they are, but they also should be aware of how they make others around them feel. If they aren't making their followers feel good about themselves or about the world around them, then they aren't truly being authentic.

Strengths and Weaknesses of Authenticity

If you work with an Authentic Woman Leader who is self-aware, is concerned about your well-being, and knows where her strengths and weaknesses lie, count your blessings, and do a dance. Talk to her about where she wants to focus her efforts and where you can help. Learn from her—learn how she has gotten to the point she is at in her career and then see if those self-reflection techniques would work for you as well. Developing authenticity is a lifelong process.

For every yin, however, there is a yang. If you are working for an Authentic Woman Leader, be prepared for feedback on your own work style or behavior you may not want to hear. She may critique your project results, or the way you went about handling a difficult customer, or the way you are working with your colleagues.

She may even point out that you have spinach in your teeth. But herein lies the difference between an Authentic Woman Leader and an authentic jerk: The Authentic Woman Leader will pull you aside and privately tell you that you have spinach in your teeth, not wanting to embarrass you in front of others. The authentic jerk will announce it in front of a crowd of people, not caring at all about your level of embarrassment.

The fundamental difference between Authentic Women Leaders and authentic jerks is that authentic jerks will not adjust their leadership style to fit those around them. We met Bill George earlier in the chapter when he defined the idea of authentic leadership for us. But ten years after he wrote his first book, he updated his thoughts on the topic because he found that leaders were using the idea of authenticity as an excuse to act like jerks. "Several authors have recently challenged the value of being authentic, claiming it is an excuse for being locked into a rigid view of one's leadership, for being rude and insensitive, refusing to change, or not adapting one's style to the situation. These arguments appear to demonstrate a fundamental misunderstanding of what constitutes an authentic leader," he says.

He clarifies, "To become authentic leaders, people must adopt flexible styles that fit the situation and capabilities of their teammates." Jerks are rigid in their delivery of leadership while Authentic Women Leaders adapt their behavior to the needs of those around them.

How to Cope with Authentic Jerks

If you are on the receiving end of feedback you don't want to hear, pause. Reflect on whether that feedback can truly improve your performance and whether the delivery was done with grace and consideration or whether it was the result of jerky behavior.

Annette is the president of an event management company and works almost exclusively with women. She loves her job and loves her team. Throughout her twenty years running the business, she has worked with some truly Authentic Women as well as some who were a little too "authentic," hurting her feelings and the feelings of those on the team. But she is the kind of Authentic Woman Leader who will pause when her feelings are hurt rather than lashing out.

"If someone did something that upset me or I thought we needed to make some changes or some tweaks, I would take the time to journal. I would really dig deep and ask myself, 'Okay, what have I done to contribute to this? Why did their behavior impact me?' I've always taken time to really question myself first. We are never 100 percent innocent, and I think one of the biggest mistakes we make is to pretend we are."

Annette goes on to say, "Now the person can be as difficult as they want to be, but the way that we react is on us, right? Once I have [reflected on] that, I will put together my talking points and I will sit down with the person in a casual conversation to say, 'Hey so actually when this happened, here is what I thought or felt.'"

I asked her what the results of these honest conversations were. "Always good. I'm not being accusatory, I'm not being 'right.' I'm just saying, 'Hey, this is what happened, and this is how it made me feel and this is why.'" And the other person respects it. They understand at the end of the day, "Wait, she really cares. Look at how invested she is."

Generally, honest conversations work with Authentic Women. If you are brave enough to share with an Authentic Woman Leader that something she said or did was hurtful, then she generally will adjust her behavior. But if she is not interested in either having honest conversations or adjusting her behavior, it may be worth a conversation with a supervisor or with your human resources department.

As always, keep conversations documented and approach the situation with data and stats to keep the emotion out of the conversation with HR/supervisors. As we discussed at the beginning of this chapter, Authentic Women Leaders can be great but it's a cautionary stereotype: people of all genders can easily and quickly cross the line into jerk-ish behavior.

Developing Your Own Authenticity

Developing your own authentic leadership style is so important; I'm adding a section to this chapter on how to develop this skill for yourself. Previous chapters have focused on how to deal with others' bad behavior. In this chapter, I'd like to add a section on how you—and I—can become better colleagues and better people in general.

As business psychologist Tomas Chamorro-Premuzic, author of *Why Do So Many Incompetent Men Become Leaders?*, says humans are generally not good at being self-aware. Becoming self-aware, then, is key to becoming an Authentic Woman Leader rather than a leader in name only. Those who are truly authentic have often done the work through self-reflection to:

- Become aware of their strengths and weaknesses when interacting with others;
- Articulate those interpersonal strengths and weaknesses; and
- Fix those interpersonal weaknesses so that they are not intentionally hurting the people around them.

It's that third step that separates those who are authentic from those who are just jerks. Authentic Women Leaders have intentionally taken a hard look at what their values are, how they have behaved under stress, and how they have treated the people around them. They then develop this self-awareness using a variety of self-reflective tools.

Many rely on journaling to really do the work to get to know themselves. Many famous leaders journal on a regular basis, including President Barack Obama, actress Jennifer Aniston, and business leader Peter Drucker.

If you are looking to start your own journaling practice, there are many websites that offer writing prompts that help you reflect on your own values. By setting aside fifteen minutes and just letting the pen move across the page to answer these questions, thoughts will often come into consciousness, giving insight to your own values and how you interact with others. Henna Inam, a C-level executive coach, offers these prompts among others as ways to get started in discovering your own authenticity at the workplace:

- What's going well now? What's creating that?
- What is challenging me now? What's creating that?
- What needs my attention?
- What strengths do I notice in myself?
- What strengths do I notice in others?

Outside of journaling, some organizations use a tool called a 360-degree feedback, in which they will ask for feedback on their performance from someone who is above them, someone who is at their same level, and someone who is below them (Society for Human Resource Management, 2009). You don't have to be in a work setting to use this type of survey to find out how you are interacting with others.

There is also an exercise that I have participated in called, "When was I at my best?" Ask friends, family, and coworkers to anonymously write about a time that you were at your best. You will be surprised at how similar individuals' responses will be, even from different people who have never met each other before. These similarities can reveal to you what your strengths and values are, particularly if you are having trouble articulating them.

Finally, some people will use leadership coaches. These coaches will challenge leaders about their decisions and about situations that are going right—and wrong—to give the leader the space to reflect on their own strengths and weaknesses. Unfortunately, coaching can be expensive. However, leadership coaching training programs often require their students to conduct a certain number of leadership coaching hours on a pro bono basis. You can offer to be coached by one of these students and receive several hours of free, often life-changing coaching at little to no cost. A quick Google search will help you find these programs at universities across the country.

Working with Authentic Women Leaders can be an amazing experience. Authentic Women Leaders are passionate about their work, practice their values, connect with the people they lead, demonstrate self-discipline, and lead with their hearts as well as their heads. However, as we've said several times, it's a fine line between authenticity and assholery. Someone who is locked into a rigid view of one's leadership, is rude and insensitive, refuses to change, and will not adapt their leadership style to the situation is an authentic jerk and is much more difficult to deal with.

Authentic Women Leadership should inspire you to develop your own authentic leadership style. Becoming an Authentic Woman Leader takes work and dedication and is never a finished process. But if you have read this far into this chapter and book, I'm guessing you have a truly authentic leader inside of you. Take the time to grow her and let her come out and lead. It will be worth it to you and those around you.

CHAPTER 9

THE QUIET WOMAN

"I had to work in an open office plan about a month ago when I was on my book tour in London. I just found it difficult to think. But then I was also struck by how much energy you need to spend just arranging your face."

—SUSAN CAIN, *QUIET: THE POWER OF INTROVERTS IN A WORLD THAT CAN'T STOP TALKING*

As I stood sobbing on the sidelines, the coaches looked at me like I was nuts. I was thirteen years old at a week-long basketball camp and we were in the middle of running drills. Not sure what to do with me, the coaches sent me to my room for some downtime.

It turned out to be just what I needed. Throughout the week leading up to that moment, I had spent twenty-four hours per day practicing, eating, sleeping, and hanging out with a few hundred other girls. For the most part it was fun, but by about Thursday of that week I needed a minute.

After an hour or so of flipping through a magazine by myself in the quiet dorm room, I was ready to get back out there to run some more drills.

I hadn't thought much about that incident until 2013 when I read Susan Cain's book *Quiet—The Power of Introverts in a World That Can't Stop Talking*. Upon reading that book, I felt seen for the first time in my life. The breakdown at basketball camp didn't mean I was a nutcase; I was just an introvert who needed to recharge her batteries in a quiet space for a few minutes. Don't get me wrong—I like people, I like being around people, but being around a lot of people for a lot of time is exhausting for me. Cain's book was so comforting in explaining that I'm not a freak because I'm not the life of the party, I'm just someone who recharges her batteries differently.

Since reading Cain's book, I have noticed other quiet women at my place of work. Assuming they were introverts like me, I gave them space but would also try to occasionally strike up conversations. Sometimes it would lead to a lovely chat, but sometimes she would just politely smile and walk away. It was then when I would start to panic. *Did I do something wrong? Does she hate me? Why is she such a bitch?* But despite my panic and assumptions, what I've found is that her quietness was usually not about me. Or at least I hoped so.

Quiet Women at Work

There are many reasons that someone might be quiet, some more nefarious than others. Like me, she could be introverted, she might be a strategist, she could be burned out, or worst of all, she could be pushing you out. But let's start with the most common and benign of possibilities.

She's an Introvert

Introverts are not antisocial (I swear, we aren't!). The main difference between introverts and extroverts is how they gain and use energy. As Susan Cain explained in an interview with *Harvard Business Review*,

> *"People often assume that introversion is related to, or means being shy, means being antisocial in some way. It's really not that at all. It has to do with how you respond to stimulation, including social stimulation. This operates at the level of the nervous system, it's not merely just a preference. Introverts really feel at their most alive, at their most energized when they're in quieter, lower key environments. Extroverts crave, need, depend on larger amounts of stimulation to feel at their best. [Introversion] is simply a preference to socialize in quieter ways."*

Introverted bosses and coworkers simply need more time to process information in a quiet way, usually alone. Sometimes they need to write out their thoughts and think through various scenarios before making decisions.

If you are working with or for someone who doesn't respond to your ideas right away, or you feel like your suggestions are falling flat, don't panic. Pause and observe. Observe whether she does the same with other people and then observe how much time she works alone. She might be simply introverted and needs time and space to process information before making decisions. Her quietness is not about you. You'll just have to be a little patient with her to get her feedback and her decisions.

She's Strategizing

In the way that social capital is the currency of the workplace, information is the power. Some women might be quietly holding on to information that could be helpful to them down the road.

Take Paul for example, a CFO and COO who has spent most of his life and career surrounded by women. "It's sort of all I know," he said during our conversation about women in the workplace.

We began discussing his experiences in working with women from the male perspective. It took him a few minutes to put his finger on what is different about the way women work, because like men, women are individuals, and each has her own working style. But through our conversation, he surmised that one skill previous female coworkers developed that his male coworkers hadn't is how to quietly use patronizing behavior—e.g., mansplaining—to their advantage.

For about eleven years before Paul arrived at his current company, his CEO did the contract negotiation with their suppliers. "I would not have tolerated the way they treated her. The suppliers were rude, 'explaining' to her how things work in their industry when nothing had changed for years and years. They always talked to her like it was her first time negotiating a contract. And she put up with it. She had to in order to get the deals done. At that time, she needed them more than they needed her."

But a funny thing started to happen. Over the past two years, the company's success exploded. The suppliers now need her company more than she needs them. Given the company's revenue, she can now take its business to any supplier she would like. But the suppliers at this point either haven't realized this fact or have chosen to ignore it, because they still talk to the CEO—and now Paul—in the same mansplaining way.

> *"I've received some of [the bad behavior] as well, because the relationship was there before I was. So often they treat me the way they've treated her. [It makes me] want to fight. I want to get aggressive, and kind of say, 'How dare you? How dare you speak to me like that?' And she will just hold me back. She'll say to me, 'Let them say what they want to say. Let them think that they have the upper hand. We both know that they don't. We both know that they are screwed if we walk away; they just have no idea.'"*

In this case, Paul's CEO was quietly strategizing, allowing the men's bad behavior to build until she had the upper hand. Women like her aren't ignoring the bad behavior; they are strategizing next steps and storing this information for future use. A little devious? Perhaps. Smart? Absolutely.

She's Burned Out

Sometimes, there are other, more personal reasons for someone you work with for being a Quiet Woman. It could be that after decades of either consciously or subconsciously leading the charge for women in the workplace, she is just burned out.

Burnout is real. Some women become burned out from playing superhero on all fronts of her life. Some women become burned out from nonstop arguing with superiors over resources at work. Some are near the end of their tenure at their current employer and have one foot out the door. For whatever reason, some bosses, coworkers, or subordinates are just checked out and couldn't care less about what is going on at work. As a result, they are uncommunicative and quiet.

You may remember Paula from chapter four when we talked about Queen Bees. Now the CEO of her own environmental education firm, Paula not only had a Queen Bee for a boss at her first internship in graduate school but had a Quiet Woman for a boss at her last internship in school. (Paula has had bad luck with bosses!)

This supervisor didn't give Paula any direction and was vague on project details. Overall, she just seemed uninterested in what Paula did. "I was constantly asking what's going on? What do you need? Where's the strategic plan? What's my job description?" said Paula. "But her response was always, 'I don't know, just go and do.'"

Paula attributes this response, however, not to her boss's personality, but to the fact that she was near the end of her career and was over it. She had been a part of a trail-blazing generation that paved the way for other women not just in academia where she and Paula worked, but in the male-dominated world of scientific academia. She had done all she could do to survive. Now she was burned out and just didn't care what Paula or anyone else did.

If your boss just seems tired, there is a good chance she has been spending much of her time and career fighting. Fighting for budgets, fighting for resources, fighting for her own career. At some point, women must choose what to fight for, and toward the end of their careers, battling at work just isn't as appealing as it once was.

She's Pushing You Out

The thing to watch out for with Quiet Women, especially Quiet Bosses, is that sometimes their quietness *can* be about you. So rather than confronting you about your mistakes or your behavior, she's hoping that if she distances herself from you, you'll take the hint and move on.

All organizations have a procedure that must be followed to fire someone, which, depending on the organization and industry, can be time-consuming, expensive, and legally risky. At the very least there must be some level of documentation that proves someone's work and/or behavior was unacceptable. There is also the possibility of a financial payout to the "bad seed," depending on her level and the type of employer, which most organizations want to avoid. All in all, it's much easier on the employer if the bad seed quits on her own.

What are some signs that you are being pushed out? According to Dominique Rogers's article "Five Subtle Signs Your Boss Is Hoping You'll Quit," many signs relate to quietness. You are no longer invited to key meetings. Your boss no longer has friendly conversations with you or no longer says hello in the morning. There is also removal: removal of assignments, removal of responsibilities, removal of projects.

If work starts going away, or if people stop talking to you, beware. We will discuss how to deal with this situation more so in just a bit. It is a tricky one.

Strengths and Weaknesses of Quiet Women

One of the reasons the Quiet Woman is at the positive end of the behavioral spectrum is because I believe that most are simply misunderstood introverts. The majority are not actively trying to push others out and those who are usually fall into the Queen Bee or Controller categories. With that in mind, benefits to working with most Quiet Women mainly revolve around the fact that she is often focused on the work and the mission of the organization. She may go about that mission differently but, unless she is burned out or pushing you out, you are likely in a good place.

The weakness of working with *all* types of Quiet Women, however, is that Quiet Women often have communication challenges, even if they are not aware of it. They usually give little feedback on your work, at least in a timely fashion. You may wander off in the wrong direction on a project and go far down the road before you are corrected. This can be frustrating, especially if you have to rework details or projects.

Specific types of Quiet Women have their own sets of strengths and weaknesses.

If She's an Introvert

Introverts make great leaders. As Adam Grant, Francesca Gino, and David A. Hofmann explain in their article "The Hidden Advantage of the Quiet Boss," decades of research have shown that extroverts are favored in hiring decisions and generally move up the ranks faster than introverts.

However, introverts make for better organizational leaders in uncertain economic situations such as the Great Recession of 2008 and the COVID-19 pandemic. *Why?* While extroverted *leaders* tend to want to be out in front and make the decisions, in uncertain times, extroverted *employees* also want to make their opinions heard. Mix the two sets of extroverts together, and all that outward energy can result in a lack of an organizational focus and direction.

Introverted leaders, on the other hand, will often take the time to listen to their constituents during times of uncertainty and consider their opinions on next steps. They are more likely to think through various scenarios and move more cautiously. As a result, the researchers show that introverted leaders garner 16 percent higher profits in times of economic uncertainty while extroverted leaders were responsible for 14 percent lower profits.

If She's a Strategizer

Strategists focus on the big picture. They likely have the best interests of you and your organization in mind. While they may not seem concerned with individuals in their work environment, their focus on the mission will often carry you along the way to group success.

The downside of Strategizers is that they sometimes leave individuals out of the loop. Because they are focused on the big picture, you can sometimes be forgotten. If you want to be more in-the-loop with what she is thinking, offer to help with small tasks and work your way up to bigger projects. But be aware that it may take time to build trust with Strategists. As with Paul's CEO, they've dealt with a lot of crap over time. She may not be open to your help right away, but start with small offerings of assistance to build trust and work your way up from there.

If She's Burned Out

At first glance, working with someone who is burned out seems to have more downsides rather than upsides. You might receive little guidance, more work might fall on your desk, and work can generally be frustrating. But where there is a void of leadership, there is opportunity.

If you enjoy your work and are interested in staying and perhaps even moving up, you can step in where your boss leaves off. You can have a conversation with her to see where she wants to focus and where you can help. If she truly is checked out, she may be relieved to know someone else is interested in filling in some of the gaps. Start with small tasks and move your way up to larger projects. Once she knows she can rely on you, you will become more visible to others around her, leading you to build your own valuable social capital.

If She's Pushing You Out

There is, unfortunately, little upside to working for someone who is quietly trying to push you out. The one positive is that those who are pushing others out are generally not in any rush to do so. Thus, you have the gift of time. There are some options listed below for you if you are being pushed out. But whatever you decide, don't wait for her to act. Take control of your career and see where other opportunities lie.

How to Cope with Quiet Women

The key to working with Quiet Women is communication, which very often, you will have to initiate. Schedule one-on-one time with her, create an agenda for meetings, and send any projects you want to review with her to her ahead of time so she has time before the meeting to process the details. Quiet Women are often uncomfortable with surprises and will internally panic if facing one. So, give her enough time to provide a response. Don't worry—she's listening, and she cares.

What to Do If She's Pushing You Out

Women being pushed out generally have two options, both of which can be pursued simultaneously. When a quiet boss is too much for you to bear, it's time to have a candid, if uncomfortable, conversation. Kim Scott outlines the reasons for, and ways to, approach these conversations in her book *Radical Candor.* She says if you truly care about your job and you'd like to stay at your organization, then it's worth facing the music.

Start by making the conversation about what behaviors you have noticed. A statement like, "I've noticed I haven't been included in some key conversations around my projects," can let her know that you are aware of her behavior but are ready to address improvements needed in your work. It's asking about her conduct without being accusatory. Remember, you can only control—and improve—your own behavior, so make the questions and the conversation about you and not your boss.

Your boss might not give you any useful feedback. ("You are doing great! I've just been having a rough time.") Or she might give you some feedback that is painful to hear. ("I've found your work to be sloppy.") Either way, document the conversation and do your best to get specific, actionable steps so you can move to change or improve your work product. And follow through on those improvements!

Offer to meet with her regularly so that you can check in to show her where work is improving. This step not only should improve your relationship with her but will protect you in case she decides you aren't following through on her requests. Adjusting your own behavior to meet organizational expectations can save your job and strengthen your relationship with your boss, even if her feedback is painful to hear.

As we discussed, Quiet Women generally take their time when pushing others out. Use that gift of time to network both within and outside of your organization with people who can connect you with other opportunities. You can also work with your HR department to see if there are other positions open within your organization that you can move into.

There are a myriad of reasons a woman—a boss, coworker, or subordinate—may be quiet. It could just be a bad day or maybe she just needs some introvert-time to recharge. But if it's ongoing behavior and you aren't sure what the motivations might be, it's worth a conversation, no matter how tough. You may or may not get information that is helpful; many people are uncomfortable in honest conversations, particularly at work. If there are concerns about your behavior, do your best to address them. As always, dear reader, remember to keep everything documented and control the only behavior you can, which is your own.

CHAPTER 10

THE MENTOR AND THE SPONSOR

"I believe we have sent the wrong message to young women. We need to stop telling them, 'Get a mentor and you will excel.' Instead, we need to tell them, 'Excel and you will get a mentor.'"

—SHERYL SANDBERG, AUTHOR OF *LEAN IN*

Anne was my sounding board as I navigated my way through my career in higher education. She gave me advice, listened to me vent, and connected me to others within the organization, helping me grow my network. Susan kept an eye on my progress, and when it came time to move up in my career, she was the one who propelled me into that next job.

However, at no time did I ever sit down with either woman and say, "Will you be my mentor?" or "Will you please sponsor me?" I was lucky enough to find these wonderful women outside of any formal mentorship program and the relationships grew organically.

Lucky being the key word. There were times earlier in my career when I was desperate for guidance or was looking for someone to brainstorm ideas with and I didn't have anyone to talk to. I didn't have access to formal mentoring programs or sponsorship opportunities, making for very lonely times. Looking back, I was fortunate enough to have had the wherewithal and privilege to move on to other organizations, where I did gain access to mentors and sponsors like Anne and Susan.

Mentorship and sponsorship relationships can be very powerful for all involved. Mentees and protégés receive career building advice while mentors and sponsors develop their own social capital... if their constituents do a good job. But therein lies the risk. Being a mentor or a sponsor comes with a higher amount of peril for women than it does men. This is why junior women have a harder time finding women mentors and sponsors as compared to junior men.

Mentorship versus Sponsorship

In the 1990s and early 2000s, women's mentorship was all the rage in business literature. Women were instructed to find mentors to help them develop their career and move up the ladder. However, mixed in with the definition of mentorship was the idea of sponsorship. Sponsorship has since been separated out into its own, more powerful act.

The difference between mentorship and sponsorship is this: mentors are sounding boards. If a woman has a question, a problem, an idea to work through, or needs to talk through an issue, a mentor is someone she can go to for feedback. Many women look to develop mentoring relationships with women in their organizations, thinking this will help propel their career forward and upward. And to a certain extent, having a mentor does help with that.

Sponsorship takes mentorship to the next level. It is mentoring plus "reaching down" and pulling someone else up. A sponsor is a senior woman willing to spend her own social capital to help a more junior woman advance in her career. A sponsor believes in another's ability so much that she will do things like recommend the protégé for promotions, committee positions, or stretch projects. The sponsor is betting that the protégé will not only grow in her own career but that the protégé's work will reflect positively upon her as well.

Whitney, a fellow higher education professional, has been lucky enough to have not just one, but three sponsors in her career. After earning her PhD in Urban Higher Education in 2018, she has gone on to simultaneously serve in two director roles at her university, reporting directly to the provost.

For those readers not familiar with the structure of higher education, these are very high-profile roles and to have two of these roles simultaneously is very impressive. Whitney attributes much of her success to Gladys, one of her three sponsors at their university.

As Gladys was moving up the ladder in her own career, she pulled Whitney up with her. When Gladys was about to begin a new role as vice president at the university, she invited Whitney to apply for her old job and advocated for her to be hired into the vacated role. Once in the role, Gladys continued to guide Whitney through her professional development, informing her which conferences she should present at and what on-campus committees she should be involved in. And when it came time for Whitney to apply to PhD programs, Gladys wrote her endorsement letter as part of her application.

Gladys even stuck with Whitney through her doctoral program. Upon Gladys's retirement as dean of students, Gladys encouraged Whitney to again follow in her footsteps and apply to her vacated position. "And if you don't get my job," Gladys told Whitney, "I want you to apply for the job that is right underneath it, because I really think you need to have an opportunity to show your talents more."

I asked Whitney what made Gladys take such an interest in her career. "It always felt like [she] had my best interests at heart," she said. "She wasn't giving me advice for my own sake. She saw something in me that I didn't see in myself, and I always appreciated that." Even when Whitney didn't feel like she had the experience or credentials to take that next step, Gladys and Whitney's other sponsors kept prodding her to take it anyway, helping Whitney grow her career.

It's one thing to advocate for another woman once, or to mentor a woman for a short period of time. It's another for a sponsor to stick with a junior woman throughout her career, as Gladys did for Whitney. I asked Whitney why she thought Gladys stuck with her for so long. After a pause, she said, "I would do what I said I was going to do. There's nothing worse than someone placing something important in your hands for you to do, and you flake on it, or you don't prioritize correctly, or you just throw it together."

Whitney's comment really hit home. It's that fear of losing one's own social capital that keeps women from sponsoring other women. Whitney was aware of this risk, so she made the effort to always do her best work, which helped her sponsors continue to believe in and sponsor her. Social capital is hard earned for women, so spending that capital by sponsoring a junior woman, like Gladys did for Whitney, is a big deal.

Mentorship, while valuable, is relatively easy; mentors just need to listen to their mentee and help her think through possible solutions. If a sponsor's protégé performs poorly, however, both the protégé and sponsor suffer the consequences. Like Whitney said, if she had flaked on any of the positions that Gladys had recommended her for, Gladys's colleagues would have questioned her judgment in addition to Whitney's abilities. Gladys would have lost some of her own hard earned social capital.

Women must choose wisely as to whom to spend their social capital on, if at all. But for all the risks of being a sponsor, mentorship and sponsorship can be a very rewarding and worthwhile experience for both parties.

Strengths and Weaknesses of Mentorship and Sponsorship

The benefits of being a mentee or protégé are obvious and numerous. For the mentee, it's helpful to have someone figure out solutions to problems. Having a mentor can help build your network and being able to talk through issues reduces stress for the mentee. For the protégé, the benefits are even greater. There is more access to stretch assignments and projects that will increase the protégé's profile. And for the protégé, a sponsor may even open a direct route to a higher position within the organization.

There are also benefits for the mentor and the sponsor. For those mentors who are looking for a fresh perspective on their own work situation, a mentee may be able to provide it. It may also be an opportunity to groom a mentee or protégé for a position on the mentor's or sponsor's team, filling a need there. And of course, there are the good feelings and ego boost that come with sharing advice and seeing someone you have mentored succeed in their own career.

The biggest benefit to sponsorship, however, is the opportunity to build your own social capital... *if* your protégé does a good job. Nicole Denson, tech portfolio and transformation director for consumer lending at JPMorgan Chase, sponsored a woman within her firm and saw the benefit to her own career as a result. "I've just promoted a diverse candidate on my team from a vice president to an executive director. The company now recognizes that I'm a serious advocate for diversity, equity, and inclusion" (JP Morgan Chase, 2021).

There is an additional drawback to mentorship and sponsorship that we have not yet discussed. Outside of formal mentorship or sponsorship programs, it is very easy for the sponsorship relationship to look like favoritism. Conscious and unconscious bias easily creeps into these relationships, particularly when these relationships are outside of a formal mentorship or sponsorship program.

Many mentors and sponsors see a bit of themselves in their mentees or protégés and want to help them avoid the mistakes and pitfalls they faced earlier in their careers. As a result, people tend to mentor and sponsor people who are like them in some way, often in gender. It's the fundamental reason men tend to sponsor other men more so than women (McKinsey, 2019).

In fact, CBS News cited a survey that investigated the impact of mentorship on men and women right after completing their MBA program. 62 percent of men in the study had found a mentor at the senior executive or CEO level at their first job after graduation, compared to 52 percent of women. Men's mentors tend to be male and higher up the corporate ladder as compared to women's mentors. Because of these male-to-male mentor relationships, the male mentees earned on average $9,260 per year more than men without mentors. Additionally, male mentees' future salaries jumped an average of 21 percent at each promotion. The women, even if they were mentored, did not realize these same benefits. Boys' clubs are real.

To combat this type of favoritism, American Express implemented a "Two Plus One" rule in their sponsorship and mentorship programs. As Sylvia Ann Hewitt explains in her book *The Sponsor Effect: How to Be a Better Leader by Investing in Others*, sponsors/mentors were required to have at least two people who don't look like them. "[At American Express] it was OK to choose someone who was very similar to you, but you'd better have a portfolio of younger talent, perhaps three people, that you are investing in, and the other two should not look like you."

How to Manage the Mentor/Sponsor Relationships

If You Are the Mentee/Protégé

If you are a mentee or a protégé, congratulations! You have struck gold! Keep that relationship strong by going above and beyond expectations. When chatting with someone you look to as a mentor, ask questions you genuinely want to know the answer to or about real challenges you are facing. As Sheryl Sandberg says in her book *Lean In*, "Leading with vague questions like, 'What is Facebook's culture like?' shows more ignorance than interest in the company since there are hundreds of articles that provide this answer."

If you are a protégé, make sure that the job, project, or assignment your sponsor is championing you for is really the one you want. Once you have it, you will have to a) do an excellent job, and b) stick around for a while to ensure she retains her social capital. If you fail to do either, she will have lost some of her social capital and you have lost a great relationship.

But what if you haven't yet found a mentor or a sponsor? The first step is to get busy within your organization. As CEO Joseph Plumeri says in Adam Bryant's 2020 article on LinkedIn, "Play in traffic. [That means] if you push yourself out there and you see people, and do things, and participate, and get involved, something happens." Mr. Plumeri said, "I tell people, just show up, get in the game, go play in traffic." Mentor and sponsor relationships tend to grow organically, so meet new people by joining committees, volunteering for projects, or joining an employee resource group.

There is also the option for joining formal mentorship programs either within your organization or within industry associations. These programs can feel a bit awkward at first; I've been on both sides of these structured mentoring relationships and conversations can at first feel forced. But given the chance, these programs not only can provide the benefit of an outsider's perspective to your challenges at work but can help you expand your network beyond your team or unit. And you never know—that could come in very, very handy one day.

You may even find a more fulfilling mentoring relationship at an organization outside of your workplace. There are many women's groups out there who offer some sort of mentorship program. And it doesn't even have to be a formal program. If you are a member of your kid's PTA, see if there are new parents who would like to be included. If you like giving back to young people, see if you can mentor an elementary or high school student. If you are looking to connect within your faith, see if your faith-based organization has a women's group to join. You may find some great relationships outside of work that can turn into mentorship or sponsorship.

If You are The Mentor/Sponsor

If you have been at your organization for a few years, you too can mentor and sponsor someone else. You don't have to be at the Sheryl Sandberg level to be a mentor. Simply giving someone new to the organization some insight as to "how things work" is mentoring. Recommending someone for an award is sponsoring. It doesn't take much—look around you to see who might need a boost and offer to help. That's all it takes.

Finally, if you truly find yourself on the outside of a mentoring or sponsoring culture and you just can't seem to break in, it may not be the environment for you. If it's important to you to have a mentor or sponsor at work and it just isn't happening where you are, then you might find a better environment somewhere else. After all, your career is in your hands, and yours alone.

CHAPTER 11

THE NEW, TRUE LEADER

———

"A true leader is someone who knows how to guide col-leagues, to really help them understand how to do it better next time versus just beating them down. A true leader sees the good in people, can see their strengths, identify weaknesses and just help them be better."

—WHITNEY MCDOWELL ROBINSON, VICE PRESIDENT FOR ENROLLMENT MANAGEMENT AND STUDENT SERVICES, TOUGALOO COLLEGE.

The following titles are the first non-paid-advertising hits on Google when I entered the phrase "working with women:"

- Why Do Women Bully Each Other at Work?—The Atlantic, 2017.
- What's a Guy to Do? Seven Ground Rules for Working with Women—The Discreet Guide, 2018.
- Tips for Men Working in a Female Dominated Workplace—Chron, 2020.

- Women in the Workplace: Why Women Make Great Leaders & How to Retain Them—Center for Creative Leadership, 2019.

Only one of those first four articles has a positive slant. Houston, we have a problem.

Where are the articles about the benefits of working with women? Why aren't there more articles about how great women are as leaders? Perhaps the writers are fishing for clicks more so than trying to help their readers, but it's clear that Queen Bees get more airtime from magazine articles to reality TV.

However, for every Queen Bee out there, there are many more True Leaders, the unsung heroes of the working world. True Leaders are the ones who lift up those around them, focus on the organization's mission, and go to bat for their team members when things get tough. If you happen to work with or for a True Leader, count your blessings. Hold on to her for dear life because she will likely give your career the boost it needs, whether you want it or not.

In thinking through my own experience, I thought about the women leaders I've had over the years. One I had early in my career was hyper-focused on the organizational mission and turned our project around from almost defunct to successful in about eighteen months. Another truly trusted me to get my job done, only interfering when I asked her to. The third has gone to the ends of the earth for her staff and successfully advocated for everyone in the office to get a pay raise when there was no money to be had in our organization.

None of these women were similar in any other particular way, really. They had different approaches to their work, had very different personalities, and worked in very different industries. However, what these women did have in common was a focus on something bigger than themselves and the willingness to bring me and my teammates along with her for the ride.

Catherine, the VP at the tech firm that we met in chapter three, was lucky enough to work with a True Leader early in her career. "I had an amazing executive vice provost at one of the universities I worked at," says Catherine. "The key with her is that she was so engaged and so secure with herself. She didn't project her insecurities onto others and allowed her team to shine in the spotlight. And that light reflected back on her." When pressed for further detail, she told the following story:

"It was just before winter break, and the executive vice provost asked me to come into her office. She told me that my team had been talking to her about my leadership. This made me a bit nervous, but she explained that my team had been remarking what great ideas I had come up with and how I had expressed some ideas for my office going forward. She then asked if I indeed had some ideas, and I said, 'Yes.' So, I nervously explained my ideas and she said, 'When we come back from break you are going to implement those ideas and I am going to help you.' I was flattered but I told her that I had never done these things before. And she said, 'But I believe that you can, and we will do this together.'" And sure enough, after break, that is indeed what happened.

So while Catherine wasn't yet confident in her own ideas, the executive vice provost saw Catherine's talent and gave her the chance to shine. She helped Catherine communicate her ideas and lead her team toward the organization's mission, and aided her in doing so along the way. And that, at any level, is true leadership.

What Is True Leadership?

In 2016, *Harvard Business Review* found that there are more CEOs named David than there are women CEOs. And David wasn't even the most popular CEO name. It was John. While this book is more about working with and for women vs. how women can climb the corporate ladder, it helps to look at the various facets of leadership to see that more women should—and could—belong in higher positions.

A 1991 study conducted by Shelley A. Kirkpatrick and Edwin A. Locke found that successful leaders, regardless of gender, had similar qualities. And while having these qualities didn't necessarily mean that a person is going to be a CEO, people with these qualities were viewed as good leaders within their organizations. These qualities include:

- drive, which includes motivation, ambition, energy, tenacity, initiative, and an orientation toward achievement.
- the desire to lead but not to seek power as an end in itself.
- honesty and integrity.
- self-confidence paired with emotional stability.
- cognitive ability.
- knowledge of the business.

Of course, many male leaders express these qualities. But in what dimensions of leadership, exactly, do women excel? How do women approach leadership differently, as compared to men?

According to Krishna Reddy at Wisestep.com, the difference lies in women's approach to decision-making and follow through. Men generally stick to what psychologists call a transactional approach. Both male and female leaders are goal-oriented, but men don't feel the need to explain their decisions regarding how a team should reach that goal. They expect employees to follow through on their own parts of the mission without question. For those employees who prefer to stay within their lane, this is a comfortable leadership style. They accept that they are responsible for the success and failure of those tasks and responsibilities within their control, but not for the success or failure of the group as a whole. "I did my part—must have been someone else's screw up."

Women, however, generally approach goals with what is called a transformational approach. Women leaders are equally as goal-oriented but choose to explain their thought process as to why they chose a certain approach. They actively work to motivate teams toward a goal, looking at success and failure as a group effort. Women tend to be more personally engaged and put teamwork and communication first.

This transformational leadership model has proven to be the most successful model in many industries. Groups with transformational leaders show better performance and employees who work in such teams feel more satisfied. These leaders motivate their followers to be more creative and empower them to develop as professionals.

Of course, then the question is, so what? Does it matter whether staff are happy if the company isn't making enough money to pay their salaries? When we start talking dollars, do women's differing leadership styles really matter? Allyson Kapin at *Forbes* says yes. She cites a study conducted by MassChallenge and Boston Consulting Group which found that, "[Start-ups] founded by women deliver higher revenue— more than two times as much per dollar invested—than those founded by men, making women-owned companies better investments for financial backers. The authors calculated that

VCs [venture capital firms] could have made an additional eighty-five million dollars over five years if they'd just invested equally in both the women- and men-founded start-ups."

So if women-led organizations ultimately generate more of a financial return on investment, why haven't investors poured more of their resources into those organizations before now? Because it is only recently that our economy has shifted to one in which women lead best: a service-based economy.

In the United States and developed countries around the world, economies either have already transitioned to or are in the process of transitioning from a manufacturing-based economy to a service-based economy (Kim 2006). Manufacturing-based economies make stuff. They rely heavily on factories to make tangible things to sell to other people. In these types of settings, the company mission is clear: sell the most things you can sell to make as much profit as possible.

People who work in manufacturing organizations know their job, their role, and then work toward the shared goal of making the product. And while human nature makes these work environments much more complex than just working toward a goal of making and selling stuff, that's pretty much the gist.

However, beginning in the mid-1990s and through 2008's The Great Recession, the US economy quickly transitioned from being a manufacturing-based economy to a service-based economy. In 1990, thirty-five states were primarily manufacturing-based, while by 2013, only seven states were still primarily focused on manufacturing. By 2013, thirty-three states became primarily dependent on healthcare and service industries, including financial services and professional services like consulting (Bureau of Labor Statistics, 2014).

A focus on service means that rather than employees interacting with machines in a factory, they are interacting with customers, clients, and with each other at work. Anytime more humans are involved, things get more complex. And when things get complex, we need leaders with high levels of something called emotional intelligence to lead the way.

Emotional intelligence, also known as EQ, is the "ability to identify and manage one's own emotions, as well as the emotions of others" (Psychology Today, 2021). Daniel Goleman, a psychologist regarded as the thought leader on the topic, says there are four components of emotional intelligence: self-awareness, managing emotions, empathy, and social skills (Goleman, 2011). Self-awareness is simply being aware of one's current emotional state, while managing our emotions means regulating appropriate reactions to stimuli in the environment. Empathy is, in general, being able to relate to and understand someone else's emotional state, while social skills dictate how to interact with others in culturally appropriate ways.

Leaders that have more EQ are more sympathetic to the plights of their colleagues or team members, while those who have less EQ tend to ignore their needs in an effort to "get the job done." When flight attendants are dealing with passengers having temper tantrums, they need pilots and leaders with enough EQ to support and advocate for them. When hotel employees have to clean up a room that guests have trashed, they need supervisors to have enough awareness to thank them for their hard work. And when healthcare providers are dealing with death all around them, they need leaders with enough empathy to provide comfort. These calm and collected actions show a high level of emotional intelligence, or true leadership.

But is EQ enough to make someone a True Leader? It's a necessary ingredient, but in today's changing economy we need people who approach decision making differently and can explain the "why" behind organizational decisions. Enter Transpersonal Leadership.

According to Greg Young, author of "Transpersonal Leadership Series: White Paper Two—Women, Naturally Better Leaders for the 21st Century," women are natural fits for this type of leadership, saying that transpersonal leaders "operate beyond the ego while continuing personal development and learning. They are radical, ethical, and authentic while emotionally intelligent and caring." Similar to the transformational leader described earlier, transpersonal leaders have the ability to:

- "Embed authentic, ethical, and emotionally intelligent behaviors into the DNA of the organization,"
- "Build strong, empathetic, and collaborative relationships within the organization and with all stakeholders," and
- "Develop a performance-enhancing culture that provides sustainability."

Young's paper then analyzes research that compares men and women on nineteen different leadership traits, including the four EQ components: self-awareness, self-management, social awareness, and relationship management, as well as attributes including service-orientation, developing others, achievement orientation, and inspirational leadership. Women outscored men on fifteen of these nineteen leadership qualities.

Women scored best on social awareness and relationship management, which also happen to be components of EQ. In other words, women excel in focusing on others' needs and the needs of the organization. Women were also stronger in serving others as well as developing others' careers within their organizations.

In short, women are more likely to be able to focus on the mission of an organization and develop those around them to be better colleagues and people. And in a service economy when we are serving other humans and not making stuff, developing staff to focus on the customer is key to an organization's success.

What True Leadership Looks Like

While True Leaders can be found around the world, one international political leader has stood out in the age of COVID-19. She has demonstrated leadership qualities beyond just emotional intelligence that can be emulated by leaders of all genders in all sectors.

The international governmental response to the COVID-19 pandemic around the world was haphazard at best. As of this writing, 4.7 million people worldwide have died (Johns Hopkins, 2021). But these deaths have not affected countries around the world equally. Very often, individual government responses to the pandemic have determined how their own populations have fared. For example, the United States has lost .2 percent of its population (Worldometer, 2021) to the disease. While that sounds like a small number, New Zealand has lost just .0005 percent of its population (Worldometer, 2021), due in no small part to its response.

The World Economic Forum began investigating why some countries fared better than others. What was the one thing that these countries, including New Zealand, along with Germany, Iceland, and Finland, have in common? They were led by women at the outbreak of the pandemic.

New Zealand's leader throughout the COVID-19 pandemic has been Jacinda Ardern. Born in Hamilton, New Zealand, in 1980, Ardern grew up in a small town that suffered from gang activity and poverty. She became inspired to use politics to help others after seeing "children without shoes on their feet or anything to eat for lunch." After earning a degree in communications, she began her political career in Tony Blair's administration in the UK in 2005 (BBC, 2020).

Upon returning to New Zealand, Ardern was elected to her first political office in 2008 and moved steadily up through the ranks until 2017 when she became the leader of the Labour Party. Then, when her party won the New Zealand elections in the summer of 2017, she moved into the role of Prime Minister by the fall of that year (Wallenfeldt, 2020).

In the following years, her country suffered crises that would challenge even the most hardened of leaders. In 2018, a gunman live-streamed the killing of over fifty people at two mosques; Ardern and her government responded by immediately outlawing semi-automatic weapons. In 2019 an earthquake killed twenty-one tourists on a remote New Zealand island; Ardern is shown comforting first responders. But at the end of 2019, she and the rest of the world began to face what we now know as the COVID-19 pandemic.

While most countries around the world decided to take a slower, "flatten the curve" approach to dealing with the pandemic, Ardern and her government decided to "go hard and go early" (Jamieson, 2020). Led by Ardern, New Zealand became one of the first countries to close its border to foreigners and impose a strict, nationwide lockdown. Its tourism-based economy took a hit, but by the end of the summer of 2020, New Zealand was also the first country to go one hundred days with no evidence of the virus. When the virus made a reappearance in August, elections were postponed and the country locked down again until October.

As of the end of 2020, New Zealand led the industrialized world in the fewest deaths due to COVID-19 and Ardern's approval rating hit record highs (BBC News, 2020).

But what did Ardern do that worked so well? After all, other countries closed their borders, enacted lockdowns, and enforced social distancing guidelines. Is there a cultural difference in New Zealand that is more accepting of these measures, or did Ardern do it differently? It turns out it was transpersonal the way that Ardern went about these measures.

1. **Service Orientation & EQ: Ardern Was Concerned About Others.** In her article "Why Do Women Make Such Good Leaders in COVID-19?," Cami Anderson says there are three factors in the pandemic that lead to early deaths: population density, exposure to those who traveled, and the date when societies shut down. The first two are out of countries' leaders' control, but the last factor is completely under the control of leadership. Those countries and cities that fared better as measured by fewest COVID-19 deaths were those that shut down earlier, even by a few days or weeks, specifically New Zealand, Germany, Iceland, and Finland. All countries led by women (Anderson, 2020).

   While it's one thing for these countries to be led by women, what drove these women leaders to shut down earlier than much of the rest of the world is women's adversity to risk. Research by the World Economic Forum has shown that women tend to be more risk-averse than men. However, the researchers found that women and men respond differently depending upon what type of risk they are facing. They suggest that while men tend to be more risk-averse when it comes to losing money, women tend to be more risk-averse when it comes to losing people. When the women leaders were faced with losing citizens within their countries to COVID-19, they acted swiftly and took more drastic action, such as shutting down borders. Male leaders around the world, more concerned with the economic impact of locking down societies, took a slower approach. The women leaders were willing to take economic risks to save peoples' lives, while male leaders were less willing to do so (Garkipati and Kambhampati, 2020). Hence, fewer deaths in countries led by women.

2. **Ardern Listened to the Experts**. Throughout the pandemic, scientists raced to understand how the virus worked, how it spread, why it was so dangerous, and how to stop it. Ardern made the decision to use the "stamp out" strategy based on the advice of her chief science advisor. Ardern had enough self-awareness (a component of emotional intelligence) to know that when it comes to the virus scientists know more than she did, and chose to take their advice for the betterment of her country. She listened to the advice of her experts, looked at her own country's medical resources and its proximity to the origin of the virus, and decided what steps were in the best interest of her country (Guy, 2021).

3. **Communications: Ardern Explained the Why and How of Their Decisions.** What really made Ardern stand out as a leader in the pandemic is the way she explained the methods in which the country would deal with the crisis. She has consistently emphasized the fact that citizens in New Zealand were in the pandemic together and she was with them, dealing with the new, restrictive lifestyle just as they were. In live chats on social media, she empathized with citizens about how disturbing the "loud honks" (nationwide emergency alert messages sent to mobile phones) must have been. She explained what it means to be in someone's bubble. She empathized with other parents about keeping kids at home rather than going to playgrounds, saying that she knows the feeling because she herself was stuck inside with a toddler. Finally, she encouraged people to not give up when things got tough being locked in their homes.

In short, Ardern was aware of how people were feeling, empathized with them, and helped steer everyone in the same direction toward the goal of eliminating the virus. Her high levels of emotional intelligence have helped her successfully lead her country through the pandemic.

Strengths and Weaknesses of Working with a True Leader

I'm sure that any office of any political leader in the world was a tough place to work in at the beginning of the COVID-19 outbreak. No doubt that Ardern's staffers argued and disagreed with each other and with her on what was in the best interest of New Zealand. But that's what happens when we care about a goal: we all want to reach that goal in the best way possible and fight to do what we feel is right. Human nature dictates, however, that we all think our way is the best. True Leaders know how to steer that energy into cooperative, goal-oriented action and the team, whether it is a team of staffers or a country of citizens, will then find they are working for a cause bigger than themselves.

The downside, if any, of working for a True Leader is that you will work hard. You may find yourself putting in long hours toward a goal that may or may not be your own. If you do find that the organization's goals are not your own, or aren't ones that you particularly care about, you find yourself asking, *Why am I doing this?* on a regular basis. And just like New Zealanders in the pandemic, you might be sacrificing more of yourself and your time than you'd like in the name of the greater good.

How to Work with a True Leader

If you are lucky enough to work with a True Leader, you have hit the jackpot. Take the time to learn from her. Use it as an opportunity to learn from her mistakes so you can develop your own leadership style to become your own True Leader. You might:

- **Observe her style.** Watch how she deals with conflict, watch how she cares for those in her charge, and watch how she runs her team or her business. Take copious notes.
- **Do what you say you are going to do.** I'm not saying become a "yes (wo)man." But when you commit to a

project or a task, do it and give it your all. If a True Leader puts her trust in you, then it's time to step up and hold on to that trust.

- **Learn from others.** Take advantage of the numerous resources on leadership out there. Read articles, books, perhaps take a class or two. Learn about leadership from others and see where the road takes you.
- **Trust yourself.** Most importantly, trust your own instincts. If you are reading this book, and more specifically, this chapter, then you are a leader in your own right. Learn from your mistakes, reflect on your own values and goals, and practice your own leadership style.

Few of us have the opportunity to work with the Jacinda Arderns of the world, but when we do, it can be a life-changing experience. Today's leaders, whether they are leading service-based organizations, manufacturing organizations, or something in between, are able to empathize with their followers and support their team members. While we like to think we can separate our personal lives from our home lives, the truth is we are all whole people who often bring our whole selves to work. Those leaders that have enough emotional intelligence to guide people through the challenges of day-to-day life are going to be the leaders that succeed. And she will likely be a woman.

CONCLUSION

———

"We will surely get to our destination if we join hands."
—AUNG SAN SUU KYI, POLITICIAN AND WINNER
OF THE 1991 NOBEL PEACE PRIZE

I have a penchant for overanalyzing things. I spend a lot of time going down rabbit holes when the answer to my question is usually fairly obvious. In the case of this book, I wanted to know the answer to a seemingly easy question but one that I found very difficult to answer:

**"How do I successfully work with other women
so going to work is enjoyable?"**

The answer, it turns out, was not an easy one to find. I began by going to the women-in-business books for answers but found them to be aimed at women working in male-dominated environments. So, I went to the more academic research. I consulted scholarly journals as well as blogs, encyclopedias, books, and conducted many interviews of my own. Eventually, I did begin to gather hints as to why women act the way they do, both positively and negatively. But rather than keep those nuggets to myself, I decided to write a book and share them with you.

After all the research, the conclusion I've come to is that women are expected to adhere to multiple sets of norms of behavior that are often in conflict with each other. System Justification Theory tells us that to retain access to resources and power women have thus far gained in our male-dominated society, we must act more like the group in power. Therefore, we begin to act more like men, particularly at our places of employment.

But when we act more like men we find ourselves shunned by the women around us. We are called Queen Bees, Controllers, Ambitious, People Pleasers, Quiet, and uncommunicative. So, we go back to acting more like society expects women to act. We become more caring, nurturing, comforting, and chatty, only to turn around and kiss our upward career trajectory goodbye.

Women are in a constant state of tug-of-war trying to live up to different sets of behavioral expectations at work. And every time we conform to one set of gendered rules, we suffer consequences with the other gender.

But there are women who have risen above the fray, who have figured out a magical balance in walking the line between too male and too female. In my research and interviews, I learned there are tools humans use to get along and work with each other, but women and men use these tools differently.

If we understand **social capital** and **trust** are built by using the tools of **self-disclosure, language**, and **emotional intelligence**—and accept the fact that we do this differently from men—then we as women can successfully work together.

Social capital is the currency of human behavior. Like money, it helps us get things done. When we have a lot of social capital, we can spend it by asking others to do things for us. If we have little social capital, few people will help us when needed. If we want others within our group to listen to us and our ideas, we need to build more social capital by performing quality work, doing favors for others, and sometimes going above and beyond what we are asked to do. Within any group of people, more social capital equals more power.

When we do what we say what we are going to do, we earn the **trust** of others. When we have the trust of a lot of people, we can build more social capital.

Unfortunately for women, trust and social capital are much more difficult to build and keep as compared to men. Women often must prove themselves over and over to build trust. Additionally, we do not carry trust and social capital from one job to the next or from one organization to the next as often as men do. We also tend to lose social capital more easily. While men's mistakes are often written off to external factors, women's mistakes are often blamed on her, reducing her social capital.

The good news is that all genders use the same tools to build trust and social capital. What is not often discussed, however, is how women and men *use* those tools differently. The tools that women use differently include:

- **Self-disclosure.** If I, as a woman, share some personal information with you, another woman, I expect you to accept that information and perhaps share some of your own information in return. This back-and-forth self-disclosure builds trust amongst people, but especially among women. The more you disclose—to a point—to another women, the more trusting your relationship with her is likely to be.

- **Language.** Women expect more explanation and more "why," particularly in female-dominated environments. We want to know why things are done the way they are, we want to explain the why behind our ideas and suggestions, and we want to know the why behind what we are being asked to do. Part of this is because women are just hardwired for more language, but part of it is that *when things go wrong, we suffer more consequences.* Again, research has shown that men's failures are often attributed to external factors while women's failures are more often attributed to her own personal defects. So, if you are working in a primarily female environment, expect to use more words and give more reasons as to why you want to go in a certain direction.

- **Emotional Intelligence.** Empathy, self-awareness, social skills, and emotional management are the components of this slippery concept called emotional intelligence. We may not recognize when someone has a lot of emotional intelligence, but we certainly recognize when someone is lacking it. Emotionally intelligent people are aware of their own strengths and weaknesses and work to address each. They know when to hold their tempers and not fly off the handle. Emotionally intelligent people are empathetic, aware of when their colleagues are struggling and work to adjust for those struggles. Those women who are aware of their own emotional intelligence and work to develop its components are more successful in the work-place, not only in moving up the ladder but in simply working with each other.

So What?

I find it a bit comical that this section is the hardest to write. I mean, so what? Now we know that women tend to use more self-disclosure, language, and emotional intelligence to build trusting relationships and social capital. What's next?

The thing is that once we know something, we have a responsibility to do something about it. If you are witness to a crime, it is your responsibility to report it. If you find the cure to cancer, it is your responsibility to share it with those who need it. And now that we have acquired knowledge about how women work, what will we—or you—do with that knowledge?

Will you choose to use brief, shortened language or will you use full explanations and instructions with others? Will you walk away from other women talking about their weekends or will you engage in conversation? Will you mentor other women starting out in their career? Will you help women build their own social capital or focus solely on yours?

The choice is yours. I hope you can use this book as a guide to improve your relationships with the women around you. I hope you can identify where your subordinates, colleagues, supervisors—and yourself—fall on the spectrum of stereotypes and learn how to work with each other's strengths, even if she is a Queen Bee. And in the end, I hope you choose to use the tools you have at your disposal beyond this book for the good of both yourself and all women.

My Take

Writing this book has been a journey of exploration. Not just because I dug deep into academic research topics such as psychology, sociology, and business, something my job does not normally call for, nor do I usually do. Not because I had an opportunity to speak with some amazing women to hear their stories about how they have navigated the world of working with women and are thriving in it, although that was amazing and inspiring. But because through this process I was able to explore my own insecurities and behavior.

While I hate to admit it, at some point in my life I have fallen into the trap of all of the stereotypes discussed. And in retrospect, each time I did it was because I was afraid, stressed, or scared. Scared that someone might find out the real me. The one who often feels she is a fraud and is afraid she might not be good enough to do the job at hand. But in talking to women who have figured it out, I have learned—or am still learning—that life is a process, and education doesn't end at graduation.

I'm still learning and growing just like everyone else. And with that idea in mind, I pledge to have the grace to be patient with others around me who are also still growing. I pledge to use the tools that I have at my disposal to lift women up around me as well. After all, a rising tide lifts all boats.

I would ask you too, dear reader, to also give yourself and those around you some grace. Take the opportunity to look at the various stereotypes and strengths described in these chapters to learn how you can become a better colleague and leader in your own right. Because that True Leader is in you; she just needs permission to be who she is and to be let loose.

ACKNOWLEDGMENTS

I would first like to thank Mike and Ben for their undying support and patience—not only during this book-writing journey but through all the crazy ideas I've pursued throughout our years together. I love you both with all my heart.

I would also like to thank my parents, Claire and Dave, for giving me the tools to succeed in life. Thank you also to Laura, Matt, Maureen, Aidan, Adam, Sandy, Holly, Savannah, and the family members yet to come. You are my inspirations.

Writing this book has been an amazing, life-changing experience. Despite the emotional highs and lows that come with the writing process, I'm so glad I did it. I'd like to thank those who helped this book become a reality along the way; it truly takes a village.

A special thank you to those who shared their stories with me, including Analia, Zoia, Marge, Lakshmi, Catherine, Paula, Emma, Lindy, Cassandra, Annette, Paul, Zayn, and Whitney.

A big shoutout to all of those who supported throughout this book-writing journey, including Jacki, Anne, Susan, Will, Larry, Erin, Deb, Julia, Sharon, Kevin, Renzo, Allynn, Melissa, Shannon, Alexander, Riva, Analia, Deborah, Stephanie, Teresa, Bonnie, Shanniece, David, Vanessa, Georgina, Mei-Ling, Paul, Sheri, Natalie, Flannery, Melissa, Ha Young, Shannon, and Tian.

Finally, a special thank you to all the folks at New Degree Press and the Creator Institute. I'd particularly like to thank my editors Cassandra Caswell-Stirling and Alayna Eberhart. You are amazingly talented women, and it was a truly a pleasure to work with you both. Thank you for cheering me on to the finish line, especially when I was ready to give up. This book absolutely would not have come to fruition without you.

Thank you to all the teachers, friends, family, bosses, and colleagues of all gender identities I have had throughout my career. I wouldn't be where I am today without you.

Lastly, I would be remiss if I didn't end with a thank you to all the women who have fought for women's rights, who have fought to be heard at home, in their social groups, and in their places of work. Regardless of your fame or fortune, your efforts have made it possible for me to have a career and to do the things that I do. I can only hope I've done the same for other women out there.

APPENDIX

———

Introduction

Shirley, Stephanie, "Why Do Ambitious Women Have Flat Heads?"
Filmed March, 2015 in Vancouver, British Columbia, Canada.
TED Video, 13:24. https://www.ted.com/talks/dame_stephanie_
shirley_why_do_ambitious_women_have_flat_heads.
(Accessed April 10, 2021)

US Department of Labor Statistics. "Women in the Labor Force:
A Databook." *BLS Reports*, April 2021. https://www.bls.gov/
opub/reports/womens-databook/2020/home.htm. (Accessed
October 18, 2021)

US Department of Labor Women's Bureau: 100 Years of Working
Women (District of Columbia, 2020), https://www.dol.gov/
agencies/wb/data/occupations-decades-100. (Accessed April
10, 2021)

Chapter 1

Ashmore, Ruth. *The Business Girl in Every Phase of Her Life*. (Philadelphia: Curtis Publishing Company + New York: Doubleday & McClure; 1898), p. 92. https://iiif.lib.harvard.edu/manifests/view/drs:2585856$6i (Accessed May 6, 2021)

Becker, J. C. (2010). "Why do women endorse hostile and benevolent sexism? The role of salient female subtypes and internalization of sexist contents." *Sex Roles*, 62, 453-467. doi:10.1007/s11199-009-9707-4Becker. (Accessed April 25, 2021)

Hayes, James. "California Divorce Reform: Parting is Sweeter Sorrow. 1970. *American Bar Association Journal*. https://www.jstor.org/stable/25725188?seq=1. (Accessed April 25, 2021)

Huffington, Arianna. *On Becoming Fearless*. New York and London: Little. Brown and Company, 2006), p. 94.

Jost, John T., and Hunyady, Orlsolya. "Antecedents and Consequences of System-Justifying Ideologies." *Association for Psychological Science*. October 1, 2005. https://journals.sagepub.com/doi/10.1111/j.0963-7214.2005.00377.x (Accessed May 8, 2021)

Kranzberg, Melvin and Michael Hannan. *Encyclopaedia Britannica Online*, s.v. "Women in the Workforce." Chicago: Encyclopaedia Britannica. https://www.britannica.com/topic/history-of-work-organization-648000/Women-in-the-workforce. (Accessed April 25, 2021)

Leibowitz, Glenn. "Why Having a Sponsor at Work Is So Critical to Your Success." *Inc*. January 31, 2019. https://www.inc.com/glenn-leibowitz/why-having-a-sponsor-at-work-is-so-critical-to-your-success.html. (Accessed October 12, 2021)

McKinsey & Company. "Women in the Workplace." September 30, 2020. https://www.mckinsey.com/featured-insights/diversity-and-inclusion/women-in-the-workplace. (Accessed April 25, 2021)

Mobly, Katharine. "Understanding The Impact of Mentorship Versus Sponsorship." *Forbes*. September 17, 2019. https://www.forbes.com/sites/forbescommunicationscouncil/2019/09/17/understanding-the-impact-of-mentorship-versus-sponsorship/. (Accessed October 12, 2021)

Nikolchev, Alexandra. "A Brief History of the Birth Control Pill." April 2016. Public Broadcasting System. https://www.pbs.org/wnet/need-to-know/health/a-brief-history-of-the-birth-control-pill/480/. (Accessed April 26, 2021)

The United States Bureau of Labor Statistics, "Labor Force Participation and Employment Rates Declining for Prime-Age Men and Women." July 2018. https://www.bls.gov/opub/mlr/2018/beyond-bls/labor-force-participation-and-employment-rates-declining-for-prime-age-men-and-women.htm. (Accessed September 4, 2021)

The United States Department of Labor Statistics. "Women in the Labor Force: A Databook." *BLS Reports*, April 2021. https://www.bls.gov/opub/reports/womens-databook/2020/home.htm. (Accessed October 18, 2021)

The United States Bureau of Labor Statistics, "Women in the Labor Force: A Databook." December 2019. https://www.bls.gov/opub/reports/womens-databook/2019/home.htm. (Accessed May 8, 2021)

The United States National Archives, "Women in the Work Force during World War II." August 15, 2016. https://www.archives.gov/education/lessons/wwii-women.html. (Accessed April 26, 2021)

The United States Equal Employment Opportunity Commission, "The Pregnancy Discrimination Act of 1978." October 31, 1978. https://www.eeoc.gov/statutes/pregnancy-discrimination-act-1978. (Accessed April 26, 2021)

The United States Justice Department, "The Equal Credit Opportunity Act." July 22, 2020. https://www.justice.gov/crt/equal-credit-opportunity-act-3. (Accessed April 25, 2021)

Zimmermann, Regula and Pascal Gygax. "Women's Endorsement of Sexist Beliefs Directed Towards the Self and Towards Other Women in General." *Men and Women in Social Hierarchies*. November 2015. https://www.researchgate.net/publication/284023169_Women%27s_endorsement_of_sexist_beliefs_directed_toward_the_self_and_toward_other_women_in_general. (Accessed April 26, 2021)

Chapter 2

Angervall, Petra, Jan Gustafsson & Eva Silfver. (2018). Academic Career: On Institutions, Social Capital and Gender, *Higher Education Research & Development*, 37:6, 1095-1108, DOI: 10.1080/07294360.2018.1477743. https://www.tandfonline.com/doi/full/10.1080/07294360.2018.1477743. (Accessed May 12, 2021)

Frankel, Lois P. *See Jane Lead: 99 Ways for Women to Take Charge at Work* (New York, NY: Hachette Book Group, 2009), p. xiii.

Helgessen, Sally, and Marshall Goldsmith. *How Women Rise: Break the 12 Habits Holding You Back From Your Next Raise, Promotion, or Job* (New York, NY: Hachette Books, Hachette Book Group, 2018), p. 98.

Ibarra, Herminia. "A Lack of Sponsorship Is Keeping Women from Advancing into Leadership." *Harvard Business Review*. August 19, 2019. https://hbr.org/2019/08/a-lack-of-sponsorship-is-keeping-women-from-advancing-into-leadership. (Accessed May 4, 2021)

OECD Insights. "Human Capital: How What You Know Shapes Your Life." Organization of Economic Cooperation and Development. February 2020. https://www.oecd.org/insights/37966934.pdf. (Accessed September 12, 2021)

Ohio State University. "Who Do You Trust? Men And Women Answer That Differently." *ScienceDaily.* www.sciencedaily.com/releases/2005/07/050718233810.htm. (accessed May 1, 2021).

Putnam, Robert. "Social Capital Primer." *RobertPutnam.com*, 2020. http://robertdputnam.com/bowling-alone/social-capital-primer. (Accessed May 12, 2021)

Zimmermann, Regula and Pascal Gygax. "Women's Endorsement of Sexist Beliefs Directed Towards the Self and Towards Other Women in General." *Men and Women in Social Hierarchies.* November 2015. https://www.researchgate.net/publication/284023169_Women%27s_endorsement_of_sexist_beliefs_directed_toward_the_self_and_toward_other_women_in_general. (Accessed April 26, 2021)

Storberg-Walker, Julia. "Borrowing From Others: Appropriating Social Capital Theories for 'Doing' HRD." *Advances in Developing Human Resources* 9, no. 3 (August 2007): 312-40. https://journals.sagepub.com/doi/abs/10.1177/1523422306304097. (Accessed May 12, 2021)

Walby, S. (2011). "Is the Knowledge Society Gendered?" *Gender, Work and Organization,* 18(1), 1-29. https://www.tandfonline.com/doi/full/10.1080/07294360.2018.1477743. (Accessed May 12, 2021)

Vsource (blog). "The Evolution of Diversity in the Workplace—2000 to 2020." August 23, 2020. https://www.vsource.io/blog/evolution-of-diversity-in-the-workplace. (Accessed September 15, 2021)

Chapter 3

Baxter, Judith, "How Speech and Language Determine Success In the Workplace," *The Guardian*, June 3, 2013. https://www.theguardian.com/women-in-leadership/2013/jun/03/speech-language-determine-success-workplace. (Accessed May 26, 2021)

Eagly, Alice and Linda Carli. "Women and the Labyrinth of Leadership." *Harvard Business Review*, September 2007. https://hbr.org/2007/09/women-and-the-labyrinth-of-leadership. (Accessed October 6, 2021)

Goleman, Daniel "Are Women More Emotionally Intelligent Than Men? It's Not Really That Simple." *Psychology Today*, April 29, 2011. https://www.psychologytoday.com/us/blog/the-brain-and-emotional-intelligence/201104/are-women-more-emotionally-intelligent-men. (Accessed May 26, 2021)

Menendez, Alicia. *The Likeability Trap: How to Break Free and Succeed as You Are.* New York City, HarperCollins Publishers, 2019, pp. 85-86.

Nash, Victoria, "Gendered Language: Women's Linguistics in the Workplace," University of North Georgia 23rd Annual Research Conference, 2018. https://digitalcommons.northgeorgia.edu/cgi/viewcontent.cgi?article=1827&context=ngresearchconf. (Accessed May 26, 2021)

Nifadkar, Sushil S., Wen Wu, and Qian Gu. "Supervisors' Work-Related and Nonwork Information Sharing: Integrating Research on Information Sharing, Information Seeking, and Trust Using Self-Disclosure Theory." *Personnel Psychology.* 2019; 72: 241-269. https://onlinelibrary.wiley.com/doi/abs/10.1111/peps.12305. (Accessed May 26, 2021)

Offermann, Lynn and Lisa Rosh. "Building Trust Through Skillful Self-Disclosure," *Harvard Business Review.* June 13, 2012.

https://hbr.org/2012/06/instantaneous-intimacy-skillfu. (Accessed May 26, 2021)

Psychology Today, "Emotional Intelligence." 2021. https://www.psychologytoday.com/us/basics/emotional-intelligence. (Accessed May 26, 2021)

Ridgeway, Cecilia, and Lynn Smith-Lovin. "The Gender System and Interaction." Annual Review of Sociology, 25, 191-216 (1999). https://www.annualreviews.org/doi/abs/10.1146/annurev.soc.25.1.191. (Accessed October 6, 2021)

Wheeless, Lawrence R. and Janis Grotz, "The Measurement of Trust and Its Relationship to Self-Disclosure," Human Communication Research. Vol 3, Issue 3, March 1977, pp. 250-257. https://onlinelibrary.wiley.com/doi/abs/10.1111/j.1468-2958.1977.tb00523.x. (Accessed May 26, 2021)

Chapter 4

Belli, Gina. "Study: Queen Bee Syndrome in the Workplace Persists." Payscale.com, April 12, 2018. https://www.payscale.com/career-news/2018/04/study-queen-bee-syndrome-workplace-persists. (Accessed May 18, 2021)

Derks, Belle, Collette Van Laar, and Naomi Ellemers. "The Queen Bee Phenomenon: Why Women Leaders Distance Themselves from Junior Women." The Leadership Quarterly, Volume 27, Issue 3, 2016. Pages 456-469. https://www.sciencedirect.com/science/article/pii/S1048984315001551. (Accessed September 19, 2021)

Drexler, Peggy. "The Tyranny of the Queen Bee," New York Times, March 6, 2013. https://www.wsj.com/articles/SB10001424127887323884304578328271526080496. (Accessed May 18, 2021)

Faniko, Klea, Naomi Ellemers, Belle Derks, and Fabio Lorenzi-Ci-
oldi. "Nothing Changes, Really: Why Women Who Break
Through the Glass Ceiling End Up Reinforcing It." *Personality
and Social Psychology Bulletin,* 2017, Vol. 43(5) 638-651.
https://a84befb0-6fb6-494f-9c77-eccaob05d681.filesusr.com/
ugd/e726ee_6b481bdb2079400e9de356e51a05788a.pdf.
(Accessed May 18, 2021)

Staack, Sherri. "Ladies, Watch Out! The Dangers of the Queen Bee
Bully Boss." *LinkedIn,* June 17, 2015. https://www.linkedin.com/
pulse/ladies-watch-out-dangers-queen-bee-bully-boss-sheri.
(Accessed May 18, 2021)

Staines, Graham, Carol Tavris, and Toby Epstein Jayaratne. "The
Queen Bee Syndrome" *Psychology Today,* January 1974, p. 57.

Henri and John Turner. "An Integrative Theory of Intergroup Conflict." *The Social Psychology of Intergroup Relations.* Monterey:
Brooks/Cole Publishing Company, 1979.

Chapter 5

APA Dictionary of Psychology. s.v. "control (n.)"
https://dictionary.apa.org/control. (Accessed September 23, 2021)

Health Essentials (blog), "How to Deal with a Control Freak."
Cleveland Clinic, May 5, 2020. https://health.clevelandclinic.
org/how-to-deal-with-a-control-freak. (Accessed May 30, 2021)

Kochanska, Grazyna and Nazan Aksan. "Development of Mutual
Responsiveness Between Parents and Their Young Children."
Child Development, November 22, 2004. 1657-1676.
https://doi.org/10.1111/j.1467-8624.2004.00808.x. (Accessed
September 21, 2021)

Leotti, Lauren A., Sheena S. Iyengar, and Kevin N. Ochsner. "Born
to Choose: The Origins and Value of the Need for Control,"

Trends in Cognitive Sciences, Volume 14, Issue 10, 2010, Pages 457-463. https://doi.org/10.1016/j.tics.2010.08.001. https://www.sciencedirect.com/science/article/pii/ S1364661310001853. (Accessed September 21, 2021)

Meyers, Psy. D., Seth. "5 Signs You Are Dealing with A Control Freak," *Psychology Today,* April 4, 2016. https://www.psychologytoday.com/us/blog/insight-is-2020/ 201604/5-signs-you-are-dealing-control-freak. (Accessed May 30, 2021)

Parrott III, Ph. D., Les. *The Control Freak.* (Wheaton, Illinois: Tyndale House Publishers, 2000), pp. 55-69.

Chapter 6

Adichie, Chimamanda Ngozi, "We Should All Be Feminists." Filmed December 2012 in London, England. TEDx video, 29:19. https://www.ted.com/talks/chimamanda_ngozi_adichie_we_ should_all_be_feminists/transcript?language=en. (Accessed June 9, 2021)

Freeland, Grant. "Indra Nooyi's Passions: People, Performance & Purpose At PepsiCo And Beyond." *Forbes,* February 24, 2020. https://www.forbes.com/sites/grantfreeland/2020/02/24/indra-nooyis-passions-people-performance--purpose-at-pepsico-and-beyond/. (Accessed September 23, 2021)

Merriam-Webster. s.v. "ambitious (adj.)." https://www.merriam-webster.com/dictionary/ambitious. (Accessed September 23, 2021)

Nooyi, Indra. "Indra's Story," *IndraNooyi.com.* 2021. https://www.indranooyi.com/meetindra. (Accessed September 23, 2021)

Riley-Bowles, Hannah, Linda Babcock, and Lei Lai, "Social Incentives for Gender Differences in the Propensity to Initiate Negotiations: Sometimes it Does Hurt to Ask." *Organizational Behavior and Human Decision Processes* 103 (2007) 84-103, November 7, 2006. https://wappp.hks.harvard.edu/files/wappp/files/social_incentives_for_gender_differences_in_the_propensity_to_initiate_negotiations-_sometimes_it_does_hurt_to_ask_0.pdf. (Accessed June 9, 2021)

Snyder, Kieran. "The Abrasiveness Trap: High-Achieving Men and Women are Described Differently in Reviews." *Fortune*, August 26, 2014. https://fortune.com/2014/08/26/performance-review-gender-bias/.

Ward, Marguerite, "Women Are Afraid to Call Themselves 'Ambitious' at Work and It's Seriously Hurting Their Careers." *Business Insider,* March 8, 2020. https://www.businessinsider.com/psychologist-recommend-strategies-ambition-women-at-work-career-goals?op=1. (Accessed June 9, 2021)

Ward, Marguerite, "Why Pepsico CEO Indra Nooyi Writes Letters to Her Employees' Parents." *CNBC*, February 1, 2017. https://www.cnbc.com/2017/02/01/why-pepsico-ceo-indra-nooyi-writes-letters-to-her-employees-parents.html. (Accessed September 23, 2021)

Chapter 7

Abrams, LCSW-R, Allison. "Overcoming the Need to Please." *Psychology Today*, October 1, 2017. https://www.psychologytoday.com/us/blog/nurturing-self-compassion/201710/overcoming-the-need-please. (Accessed May 30, 2021)

Biography.com. "Sheryl Crow Biography." April 2, 2014.

https://www.biography.com/musician/sheryl-crow. (Accessed September 25, 2021)

Braiker, Harriet. *The Disease to Please*, (New York: McGraw Hill, 2001), pp. 7-8.

Clayton Lea, Tony. "Sheryl Crow: 'Cancer Rebooted the Way I Looked at My Life'." *The Irish Times*, October 16, 2014. https://www.irishtimes.com/culture/music/sheryl-crow-cancer-rebooted-the-way-i-looked-at-my-life-1.1961971. (Accessed September 25, 2021)

IMDB.com. "Sheryl Crow Awards." 2019-2021. https://www.imdb.com/name/nm0002028/awards. (Accessed September 25, 2021)

Kushner, Robert F. and Seung W. Choi. "Prevalence of Unhealthy Lifestyle Patterns Among Overweight and Obese Adults." *Obesity*, 2010. 18, 1160-1167. doi:10.1038/oby.2009.376. (Accessed October 13, 2021)

Long, Psy. D., Colleen. "When You're Afflicted with the Disease to Please." *Psychology Today*, January 9, 2015. https://www.psychologytoday.com/us/blog/the-happiness-rx/201501/when-youre-afflicted-the-disease-please. (Accessed May 30, 2021)

Saunders, Elizabeth Grace. "How to Work for a Boss Who Has a New Idea Every 5 Minutes." *Harvard Business Review*, November 16, 2018. https://hbr.org/2018/11/how-to-work-for-a-boss-who-has-a-new-idea-every-5-minutes. (Accessed May 30, 2021)

Schreffler, Laura. "Sheryl Crow: 7 Things That Having Breast Cancer Taught Me." *Haute Living*, October 6, 2016. https://hauteliving.com/2016/10/sheryl-crow-7-things-that-having-breast-cancer-taught-me/622277. (Accessed October 13, 2021)

Chapter 8

Chamorro-Premuzic, Tomas. "The Dark Side of Authentic Leadership," *Forbes*, October 28, 2020, https://www.forbes.com/sites/tomaspremuzic/2020/10/28/the-dark-side-of-authentic-leadership/. (Accessed May 16, 2021)

Chan, Katie. "Oprah Winfrey: A Personal Brand Grounded in Authenticity." *Medium,* February 19, 2021. https://medium.com/high-profile-magazine/oprah-winfrey-a-personal-brand-grounded-in-authenticity-c93745b09390. (Accessed September 27, 2021)

George, Bill. "Truly Authentic Leadership." *US News and World Report*, October 30, 2006. https://www.billgeorge.org/articles/truly-authentic-leadership. (Accessed April 2, 2021)

George, Bill. "The True Qualities of Authentic Leaders," *Forbes*, Nov 10, 2015. https://www.forbes.com/sites/hbsworkingknowledge/2015/11/10/the-true-qualities-of-authentic-leaders/. (Accessed October 16, 2021)

Herminia Ibarra, "Yes, Good Leaders Are Authentic Leaders—But Here's What That Actually Means," *Ideas.Ted*, February 16, 2021. https://ideas.ted.com/yes-good-leaders-are-authentic-leaders-but-heres-what-that-actually-means. (Accessed May 22, 2021)

Inam, Henna. "To Be An Effective Leader Keep A Leadership Journal," *Forbes*, April 2, 2017. https://www.forbes.com/sites/hennainam/2017/04/02/to-be-an-effective-leader-keep-a-leadership-journal/. (Accessed May 23, 2021)

Lloyd, Joan. "360-Degree Feedback Is Powerful Leadership Development Tool." *Organization and Employee Development*, Society for Human Resource Management, July 13, 2009. https://www.shrm.org/resourcesandtools/hr-topics/organizational-and-employee-development/pages/360-degreefeedback.aspx. (Accessed October 20, 2021)

Winfrey, Oprah. "Every Person Has a Purpose." *Oprah.com*, November 2009. https://www.oprah.com/spirit/how-oprah-winfrey-found-her-purpose. (Accessed September 27, 2021)

OWN. "How a Gang of Skinheads Forever Changed the Course | The Oprah Winfrey Show | Oprah Winfrey Network." *Oprah Winfrey Network*. January 2015. https://youtu.be/5BRDSvO_eDA. (Accessed September 27, 2021)

Chapter 9

Cain, Susan. "The Power of the Introvert in Your Office," *HBR Ideacast*, July 19, 2012. https://hbr.org/podcast/2012/07/the-power-of-the-introvert-in. (Accessed May 24, 2021)

Grant, Adam, Francesca Gino, and David A. Hofmann, "The Hidden Advantages of Quiet Bosses," *Harvard Business Review*, December 2010. https://hbr.org/2010/12/the-hidden-advantages-of-quiet-bosses. (Accessed May 24, 2021)

Rodgers, Dominique. "Five Subtle Signs Your Boss Is Hoping You'll Quit," *Fast Company*, February 7, 2017. https://www.fastcompany.com/3067939/five-subtle-signs-your-boss-is-hoping-youll-quit. (Accessed May 24, 2021)

Scott, Kim. *Radical Candor: How to Get What You Want By Saying What You Mean*. (New York: St. Martin's Press, 2017), pp. 19-42.

Chapter 10

Bryant, Adam. "How To Get A Sponsor, Be A Sponsor, And Make The Most Of The Relationship." *LinkedIn*, July 17, 2020. https://www.linkedin.com/pulse/how-get-sponsor-make-most-relationship-adam-bryant/. (Accessed September 29, 2021)

Hewitt, Sylvia Ann. "The Surprising Benefits of Sponsoring Others at Work." Interview by Allison Beard. *HBR IdeaCast,* HBR.org, June 18, 2019. Audio, 26:21. https://hbr.org/podcast/2019/06/the-surprising-benefits-of-sponsoring-others-at-work. (Accessed September 29, 2021)

Ibarra, Herminia. "A Lack of Sponsorship Is Keeping Women from Advancing into Leadership," *Harvard Business Review,* August 19, 2019. https://hbr.org/2019/08/a-lack-of-sponsorship-is-keeping-women-from-advancing-into-leadership. (Accessed June 15, 2021)

JP Morgan Chase (blog). "The Importance of Mentors and Sponsors in Career Development." 2021. https://www.jpmorganchase.com/news-stories/the-importance-of-mentors-and-sponsors-in-career-development. (Accessed September 29, 2021)

Krivkovich, Alexis and Marie-Claude Nadeau. "The Link Between Sponsorship and Risk-taking for Women in Financial Services." *McKinsey & Company,* May 22, 2019. https://www.mckinsey.com/industries/financial-services/our-insights/banking-matters/the-link-between-sponsorship-and-risk-taking-for-women-in-financial-services. (Accessed October 20, 2019)

Sandberg, Sheryl. *Lean In* (Alfred A. Knopf: New York, 2013), p. 68, 71.

Weisul, Kimberly. "Why Mentoring Helps Men More Than Women." *CBS News,* March 25, 2011. https://www.cbsnews.com/news/why-mentoring-helps-men-more-than-women. (Accessed September 29, 2021)

Chapter 11

Anderson, Cami. "Why Do Women Make Such Good Leaders During COVID-19?" *Forbes,* April 19, 2020. https://www.forbes.com/

sites/camianderson1/2020/04/19/why-do-women-make-such-good-leaders-during-covid-19/. (Accessed June 5, 2020)

BBC News. "Jacinda Ardern: New Zealand's Prime Minister." October 17, 2020. https://www.bbc.com/news/world-asia-54565381. (Accessed June 5, 2021)

Bureau of Labor Statistics, US Department of Labor, *The Economics Daily*, Largest industries by state, 1990-2013 at https://www.bls.gov/opub/ted/2014/ted_20140728.htm. (visited June 5, 2021).

Crittenden, Jennifer. "What's a Guy to Do? Seven Ground Rules for Working with Women." *The Discreet Guide*, 2018. https://www.discreetguide.com/articles/whats-a-guy-to-do-seven-ground-rules-for-working-with-women. (Accessed October 14, 2021)

Friedman, Uri. "New Zealand's Prime Minister May Be the Most Effective Leader on the Planet," *The Atlantic*, April 19, 2020. https://www.theatlantic.com/politics/archive/2020/04/jacinda-ardern-new-zealand-leadership-coronavirus/610237/. (Accessed June 5, 2021)

Garikipati, Supriya and Uma Kambhampati, "Women Leaders Are Better at Fighting The Pandemic," *World Economic Forum*, July 28, 2020. https://www.weforum.org/agenda/2020/07/women-leaders-policymakers-covid19-coronavirus. (accessed June 5, 2021)

Goleman, Daniel. "Are Women More Emotionally Intelligent Than Men?" *Psychology Today*, April 29, 2011. https://www.psychologytoday.com/us/blog/the-brain-and-emotional-intelligence/201104/are-women-more-emotionally-intelligent-men. (Accessed June 5, 2021)

Guy, Jack. "Jacinda Ardern Didn't Feel Like She Was 'Tough Enough' for A Career in Politics," *CNN*, June 3, 2021. https://www.cnn.com/2021/06/03/asia/axe-files-jacinda-ardern-interview-scli-intl/index.html. (Accessed June 5, 2021)

Jamieson, Thomas. "'Go Hard, Go Early': Preliminary, Lessons From New Zealand's Response to COVID-19." *The American Review of Public Administration*, July 13, 2020. https://doi.org/ 10.1177/0275074020941721. (Accessed October 20, 2021)

Johns Hopkins University Coronavirus Resource Center Dashboard. https://www.arcgis.com/apps/dashboards/bda7594740fd-40299423467b48e9ecf6. (Accessed September 29, 2021)

Johnson, Stefanie K., David R Hekman, Elsa T. Chan. "If There's Only One Woman in Your Candidate Pool, There's Statistically No Chance She'll Be Hired." *Harvard Business Review*, April 26, 2016. https://hbr.org/2016/04/if-theres-only-one-woman-in-your-candidate-pool-theres-statistically-no-chance-shell-be-hired. (Accessed June 15, 2021)

Kapin, Allyson. "10 Stats That Build the Case For Investing In Women-Led Startups." *Forbes*, January 28, 2019. https://www.forbes.com/sites/allysonkapin/2019/01/28/10-stats-that-build-the-case-for-investing-in-women-led-startups/. (Accessed September 29, 2021)

Khazan, Olga. "Why Do Women Bully Each Other at Work?" *The Atlantic*, August 3, 2017. https://www.theatlantic.com/magazine/archive/2017/09/the-queen-bee-in-the-corner-office/534213/. (Accessed October 14, 2021)

Kim, Hyun-Jeong. "The Shift to the Service Economy: Causes and Effects." *Institute for Monetary and Economic Research, The Bank of Korea*, July 7, 2006. https://faculty.washington.edu/karyiu/confer/seoul06/papers/kim_hj.pdf. (Accessed September 29, 2021)

Kirkpatrick, Shelley and Edwin Locke. (1991). "Leadership: Do Traits Matter?" *The Executive*, 5. (1991) 48-60. 10.2307/4165007. https://www.researchgate.net/publication/262082812_Leadership_Do_Traits_Matter. (Accessed June 15, 2021)

Leading Effectively Staff. "Women in the Workplace: Why Women Make Great Leaders & How to Retain Them." Center for Cre-

ative Leadership, December 2, 2019. https://www.ccl.org/
articles/leading-effectively-articles/7-reasons-want-women-
workplace. (Accessed October 14, 2021)

Meier, Dr. Kelly S. "Tips for Men Working in a Female-Dominated
Workplace." *Chron*, October 7, 2020. https://work.chron.com/
tips-men-working-femaledominated-workplace-2922.html.
(Accessed October 14, 2021)

Psychology Today. "Emotional Intelligence" 2021.
https://www.psychologytoday.com/us/basics/emotional-
intelligence. (Accessed October 14, 2021)

Reddy, Krishna. "Male vs Female Leadership: Differences and
Similarities." *Wisestep*, 2018. https://content.wisestep.com/
male-vs-female-leadership/. (Accessed June 15, 2021)

Wallenfeldt, J. "Jacinda Ardern." *Encyclopedia Britannica*, October
21, 2020. https://www.britannica.com/biography/Jacinda-
Ardern. (Accessed June 5, 2021)

Young, Greg. *Transpersonal Leadership Series: White Paper Two:
Women, Naturally Better Leaders for the 21st Century*. Abington,
United Kingdom: Routledge, Taylor & Francis Group, 2018.
https://www.routledge.com/rsc/downloads/CHBUSISP1801_
Transpersonal_Leadership_WP2.pdf. (Accessed June 5, 2021)

Worldometer. https://www.worldometers.info/world-population/
us-population/. (Accessed September 29, 2021)

Worldometer. https://www.worldometers.info/world-population/
new-zealand-population/. (Accessed September 29, 2021)

Conclusion

Stewart, Whitney. *Aung San Suu Kyi: Fearless Voice of Burma*.
Minneapolis, Minnesota: Lerner Publications Company/Min-
neapolis. 1997.